PEAK DOORWAYS TO EMANCIPATION

GREAT COMPLETION TEXTS ON INTRODUCTION TO THE NATURE OF MIND AND THOROUGH CUT FROM THE COLLECTED WORKS OF SHAKYA SHRI

BY TONY DUFF

PADMA KARPO TRANSLATION COMMITTEE

This text is secret and should not be shown to those who have not had the necessary introduction and instructions of the Thorough Cut system of Dzogchen meditation. If you have not had the necessary instructions, reading this text can be harmful to your spiritual health! Seal. Seal. Seal.

First edition, June 2008
ISBN: 978-9937-9031-9-6

Janson typeface with diacritical marks and
Tibetan Classic typeface
Designed and created by Tony Duff
Tibetan Computer Company
http://www.tibet.dk/tcc

Produced, Printed, and Published by
Padma Karpo Translation Committee
P.O. Box 4957
Kathmandu
NEPAL

Web-site and e-mail contact through:
http://www.tibet.dk/pktc
or search Padma Karpo Translation Committee on the web.

CONTENTS

INTRODUCTION

The Texts

Shakya Shri was one of the great gurus of the Drukpa Kagyu lineage in Kham, Eastern Tibet, in the latter half of the nineteenth century. He was well-known for his intense practice and the realization that came from it. He was particularly famous and is still revered for having mastered both Mahamudra and Great Completion practices. He was both accomplished and knowledgeable to the point where he could teach his disciples according to their karmic propensities. For some, he taught the pure Mahamudra path of the Drukpa Kagyu; for some, he taught the pure Great Completion path of the Nyingma which had found its way into Drukpa Kagyu. The synthetic approach is clearly seen in the first text of this collection. The pure approach of Great Completion is seen in the second text, which is a mind terma of his own collection of termas or revealed treasures.

The Kagyus in general have two approaches to realizing Mahamudra: graded and sudden. The graded approach, called "The Four Yogas of Mahamudra", came through the Indian siddha Shantipa and is taught in all Kagyu schools. In four steps it starts with shamatha, goes to vipashyana, unifies the two, and finally gets to the ultimate meaning of non-meditation. The sudden approach, called "Essence Mahamudra", is not found in all Kagyu schools. It is very similar to the Thorough Cut practice of Great Completion.

The Drukpa Kagyu maintain that they follow the approach of Shantipa in particular and that they do not even have the words "Essence Mahamudra in their system. This is clearly stated by present day masters of the lineage, for example, Dorzong Rinpoche and others of the present day East Tibetan Drukpa Kagyu lineage. What they say is true, though the third Khamtrul Rinpoche wrote a very short text called *Refined Gold* that presents the practice of essence Mahamudra even though the name "essence Mahamudra" is not used in it.

The Khamtrul Rinpoches were the principal holders of the Drukpa Kagyu in East Tibet. They inherited the pure Drukpa Kagyu lineage that came down through Lingje Repa but they also revealed many treasures according to the Nyingma and incorporated these into the practice of the East Tibetan Drukpa Kagyu. Shakya Shri was a disciple of the sixth Khamtrul Rinpoche Tenpa'i Nyima [1849–1907] (whose name is mentioned in the colophon of the first text in here). Thus he inherited the gradual approach of Mahamudra and the sudden approaches of Great Completion from his guru.

As mentioned earlier, he became highly accomplished and learned in both systems as passed down through his guru. In addition, he revealed a set of mind treasures of Great Completion teachings called *Accomplishing Guru Great Bliss*. That anthology of texts belongs to the "very secret"[1] level of Great Completion teaching. This name is a synonym for the innermost level of Great Completion teachings, also known as "Nyingthig". The second text in here is from that anthology and so, as it says at the beginning of the text, is of the "very secret" type of teaching.

Shakya Shri became very famous in his tradition for teaching a combined approach to reality using the Mahamudra system that he received from the Eastern Drukpa Kagyu and the Great Completion system that he received from his guru and from his personal revelations as mentioned just above.

The combined approach is evident in the first text here, which he wrote for one of his disciples. The text starts out with an invocation that is pure Great Completion. Following that, the practice is taught in a gradual way. First he teaches shamatha. He does that with the Mahamudra style of shamatha teaching and then incorporates some Great Completion teaching by presenting a couple of the "Parting into Sides" practices in which a HŪṂ letter is used as the basis for developing shamatha. From there, the practice of shamatha that leads into vipashyana is taught using "abiding, moving, and knowing" which is a hallmark teaching of gradual Mahamudra as passed on by the Kagyu. Some elements of that explanation, such as when he writes "Due to having merged the three of abiding, moving, and knowing …" are special teach-

[1] Tib. yang gsang. Meaning the innermost level of the upadeśha section of the Great Completion Teaching.

ings found in the Drukpa Kagyu. At the very end of the teaching on vipashyana, he makes the leap to the ultimate in one paragraph. First, he mentions common awareness which, as the mind of the buddhas, is something that all beings have. This is Kagyu way of talking. Then he immediately goes on to mention the introduction to mind which is the essential feature of the approaches found equally in Mahamudra and Great Completion explanations. From there, he smoothly shifts to the practices of "very secret" Great Completion—the pair of practices called Thorough Cut and Direct Crossing. He finishes his explanation with one sentence that captures the teachings of very secret Great Completion in particular, which is the buddhahood of attaining a rainbow body in this very life. In that way, Shakya Shri emphasizes the standard, Mahamudra approach of the Drukpa Kagyu for his disciple, but wraps it all up in a container of ultimate Great Completion approach. He concludes with ancillary advice that is always part of these teachings. The advice on extracting the profit and so on, while not unique to Mahamudra, has a ring to it here that echoes the Mahamudra way of talking as passed on through the Kagyu.

The second text is pure Great Completion. It does not show the combined approach that Shakya Shri is famed for but does show that he was fully connected to the Great Completion teaching. As mentioned earlier, Shakya Shri revealed a set of mind treasures of Great Completion teachings called *Accomplishing Guru Great Bliss*. That anthology consists of a number of yidam practices at the Ati level of practice. These centre around a manifestation of Guru Rinpoche called "Guru Great Bliss", hence the name of the anthology. The anthology is also known for having a pithy text each on the

The principal lineage teachers of innermost Great Completion as it came into Tibet including Garab Dorje, the source of the teaching in general and the Three Lines teaching in particular. Garab Dorje above left, Manjushrimitra above right, Vimalamitra below left, Shri Singha below right of Padmasambhava in the centre. Mural on the wall of Dzogchen Monastery, Tibet, 2007. Photograph by the author.

two main practices of the very secret level of Great Completion teaching—the pair of practices called Thorough Cut and Direct Crossing. The Thorough Cut text is included in Shakya Shri's *Collected Works*[2] but the Direct Crossing text is not. Presumably the latter is just too secret to let out. The Thorough Cut text is the second text translated here. The colophon at the end shows that the text is very secret. It also shows that it was an on the spot record of a revelation as it occurred. Shakya Shri connected with the space of reality that the text presents and the meaning opened to him. He saw the meaning as it presented itself, interpreted it into and spoke it in Tibetan language, and his scribe wrote it down on the spot. At the end, the doorway closed and the revelation, and text with it, ended.

Our Supports for Study

I have been encouraged over the years by all of my teachers and gurus to pass on some of the knowledge I have accumulated in a lifetime dedicated to the study and practice, primarily through the Tibetan Buddhist tradition, of Buddhism. On the one hand they have encouraged me to teach. On the other hand, they are concerned that, while many general books on Buddhism have been and are being published, there are few books that present the actual texts of the tradition. They and many other, closely involved people have encouraged me to make and publish high quality translations of individual texts of the tradition.

---

[2] Tib. gsung 'bum.

In general, we have published a wide range of books that present the important literature of Tibetan Buddhism. In particular, the author of this book was one of the important figures in the transmission of both the Great Completion and Mahamudra teachings in Tibet. We have published many of the important texts of both systems, all carefully selected to inform about a particular aspect of the teaching, and all of these will be useful as supports for this book. The book called *Hinting at Dzogchen* are very applicable because it contains teachings of Tsoknyi Rinpoche, whose lineage of Drukpa Kagyu teachings descend directly from Shakya Shri. The book covers a wide variety of the topics that are essential to understanding the most profound topics contained in this book. On the other hand, many of our other books mention the topics of introduction and rigpa practice and this book was specifically put together to be a support for all of those publications.

All in all, you will find many books both for free and for sale on our web-site, all of them prepared to the highest level of quality. Many of our books are available not only on paper but as electronic editions that can be downloaded, and all of them are prepared to the highest level of quality. We encourage you to look at our web-site to see what we have; the address is on the copyright page at the front of this book. Major book sellers also carry our paper editions.

It has also been a project of ours to make tools that non-Tibetans and Tibetans alike could use for the study and translation of Tibetan texts. As part of that project, we prepare electronic editions of Tibetan texts in the Tibetan Text input office of the Padma Karpo Translation Committee and make them available to the world. Tibetan texts are often corrupt so we make a special point of carefully correcting our work before making it available through our web-site. Thus, our electronic texts are not careless productions like most Tibetan texts found on the web but are highly reliable editions that can be used by non-scholars and scholars alike. Moreover, many of the texts are free. The Tibetan texts for this book are available for download as a free, electronic editions. They are also included at the back of the book as aids to serious study.

Our electronic texts can be read, searched, and so on, using our Tibetan software. The software can be used to set up a reference library of these texts and then used to read and even research them quickly and easily. The software, called TibetD and TibetDoc, has many special features that make it useful not only for reading but also for understanding and even translating texts. One key feature is that you can highlight a Tibetan term in a text then look it up immediately in any of our electronic dictionaries. We suggest the highly acclaimed *Illuminator Tibetan-English Dictionary* as the best dictionary for the purpose. As with all of our publications, the software and electronic texts can be obtained from our web-site whose address is on the copyright page at the front of the book.

Health Warning

The two texts here are about subjects that are usually kept secret. The colophon of the second one makes very clear just how secret the material of the text is and how few people will be able to really understand it. Therefore, I have translated the two texts as they are, providing enough notes so that someone who does understand the meaning could understand the translation without mistake. However, I have deliberately not given any further explanation of or commentary to the meaning. Anyone who has had these teachings in person will be able to understand them or at least go to their teacher and ask for an explanation. Anyone who has heard these teachings in person from a qualified teacher, and especially who has had the introduction to the nature of mind[3] around which the teachings hinge, please use and enjoy the texts as you will. However, if you have not heard these teachings and if you have not had a proper introduction to the nature of your mind, you would probably be better off not reading this book but seeking out someone who could teach it to you. These days there are both non-Tibetans and Tibetans who can do that for you and who are fairly readily available in many countries across our planet. In short, the contents of this book could be dangerous to your spiritual health if you are not ready for it, so exercise care.

I have many times in the last few years run into young men who are extremely confident of their understanding of the meaning of these profound systems but who just spout words that they have read in books. The solidity of their minds is noticeable. Unfortunately, they have read the books and know the words but have not contacted the inner meaning that the books are intended to be merely a pointer towards.

---

[3] Introduction to the nature of mind is mostly mis-translated these days as "pointing out" instruction.

Lotsawa Tony Duff
June 22nd, 2008
Swayambhu,
Nepal

“OPENING THE DOOR TO EMANCIPATION” A VERY ABBREVIATED UNCOMMON GUIDE[4] TO MIND

by Drubwang Shakya Shri

NAMO GURU

I pay homage with highly respectful three doors to the feet of the Lord of the Families, Tenpa’i Nyima Rinpoche[5], who is

[4] Tib. sems khrid. “Guide to mind” is a common technical term in use in the higher tantras to indicate instruction that leads you to a direct understanding of your mind. It is uncommon in the sense that it deals not with the surface aspect mind, which is the dualistic mind of beings in samsara, but with its innate enlightenment. In this case, it was a very short instruction given, as it clarifies in the colophon, at the request of one of his dharma friends of the time. It presents the instruction following the Nyingma Great Completion (Dzogchen) approach but mixes a lot of Drukpa Kagyu Mahamudra with it.

[5] Tenpa’i Nyima [1849–1907] was Shakya Shri’s root guru, the sixth Khamtrul Rinpoche. The Khamtrul’s were the heads of a Drukpa Kagyu lineage in Kham and their monastery was called Khampagar.

not separate from the origin protector[6]. Here, I will write a little about the way of preserving mind's actuality; may it blessing those who have requested the command[7]!

It is in two parts, the preliminaries and the main part.

1. The Preliminaries

First, there are the common preliminaries of training rational mind[8] to the point of trusting in the difficulty of finding leisure and connection, death and impermanence, karmic cause and effect, and the disadvantages of cyclic existence, then meditating on them until attachment to cyclic existence has been turned back. The uncommon preliminaries of taking refuge in dharma combined with prostrations, meditation and

---

[6] The origin protector is one of many names for the *origin*al state of enlightenment innate to each person which is personified in Nyingma as the *protector* Samantabhadra and in Kagyu as Great Vajradhara.

[7] Commands here means the words of the tradition, which in the Kagyu have always been given as commands for practice.

[8] Tib. blo. Rational mind is one of several, specific terms for mind in Buddhist terminology which, unfortunately, is usually just translated as mind. Rational mind is a name for dualistic mind given from the perspective that it always works through conceptual name tags in a process of judging this against that. It literally does make ratios. In Mahamudra and Great Completion, it is a pejorative term in the sense that it always implies dualistic, samsaric mind and not the essence of that mind, which is free of conceptuality, does not work in conceptual rations, and is the innate enlightenment of all sentient beings.

recitation of Vajrasatva, mandala, and guru yoga are to produce the signs as usual of Great Completion[9].

2. The Main Part

The main part further has the parts of body posture, bringing down the guru's blessings, and the technique for looking at mind[10].

---

[9] This simply means that the uncommon preliminaries are done for the usual purpose within the larger system of Great Completion. This usual purpose will be understood by anyone who has had the instructions on these preliminaries.

[10] As mentioned above, there are several terms in the Indian and Tibetan languages for naming mind in its various modes and aspects. When reading the texts in these languages, the use of these various terms makes it very clear to the reader what is being talked about. However, in English, we have only very few words for mind and translations all too often simply translate the various terms with the one English word, "mind". In doing so, the meaning so clear in the original becomes totally lost to the reader. This is particularly a problem with the kind of material being presented here because it relies on the use of these terms to make the needed distinctions. Therefore, I have found a set of English terms for these various terms for mind and always use them as required. The term "mind" is always used to translate the Sanskrit "citta" which is "sems" in Tibetan. This term specifically means the samsaric mind in general which is a product of ignorance and which is a very complex apparatus that functions in a dualistic way. When you see "mind" by itself, that is what is being referred to. The tradition uses the term "entity of mind" or "mind's entity" to indicate the original form of mind, what it

(continued...)

First, the body is to be put into the Seven Dharmas of Vairochana.

Second, bringing down the guru's blessing is as follows. Visualize yourself instantly as Chemchog[11] male and female with the entity, your root guru[12], on a sun and moon seat

---

[10](...continued)
actually is, prior to ignorance coming along and producing the massively complex samsaric "mind". There is one word in Sanskrit and Tibetan that equally has the meanings "entity" and "essence" and when that word is used, both connotations appear to the reader. In English, unfortunately, we have two words, not one. In this text, I have used "entity" for that word. When you read it understand that it means, "the thing itself, what it actually is" and also "essence". For example, "the entity of mind" is the very fact of what mind is before it becomes complicated due to ignorance. Mind, which is the product of ignorance, is a superfice that appears over the actual "entity of mind". The paths of Mahamudra and Great Completion are exactly to the point of removing the ignorant process of mind so that one returns to the uncomplicated essence of that mind, which is the very entity of what actually is. These are the words of the tradition and how they are used.

[11] Skt. Mahottara, Tib. che mchog. One of the yidams of the eight great practices brought into Tibet by Guru Rinpoche.

[12] Here "entity" has a specific meaning. The guru is the very fact, the very entity of enlightenment. He gives you empowerment and the practice of a yidam for you to return to that enlightenment. When you practise the yidam, as you are doing here by visualizing yourself as the yidam, you are merely the superfice whereas the guru is the thing itself that you are trying to get to
(continued...)

above the crown of your head. In the form of Samantabhadra, with azure blue body[13] in dharmakaya style[14], in equipoise mudra, and adorned by the marks and illustrative signs[15], he is conjoined with the female, dharmadhatu Samantabhadri who is white. They are seated in the midst of a space filled with the five types of rainbow light. Supplicate from the very core of your heart and, with that, repeat this:

"To this, the outer refuge protector, kind guru, lord,
I prostrate with highly respectful three doors.
Bless me so that alpha purity rigpa-emptiness is met
in self-introduction and
The liveliness of the four appearances of Direct
Crossing goes through to completion so that

---

[12](...continued)
through the yidam practice. Therefore, you visualize yourself as the yidam and that is the superfice, and you have your guru on top of your head, and that the very entity of what you are trying to get to in your practice. Thus, your visualization is complete because you have both.

[13] Tib. mthing ga. These days most translations just skip over the detail contained in this word and translate it as "blue". However, it is a very specific blue, azure blue, and is connected with many oral instructions in the practices that lead to direct sight of reality, especially in the Nyingma system.

[14] Dharmakaya style is that the deities are naked, which is a symbol of the dharmakaya being without anything extraneous to the state of utter realization of reality.

[15] The thirty-two marks as they are properly called and eighty illustrative signs as they are properly called, of a buddha.

The rainbow body, a heap of light, is produced.[16]"

Supplicate assiduously that way until the hairs of your body stand on end and tears flow down your face. After that,

"From a white OṂ at the forehead of the glorious guru
White light radiating in chains
Enters the white bindu at my forehead and
That bindu becomes vividly marked with an OṂ letter.

---

[16] This verse has profound meaning and much could be written about it. There are two main practices of the innermost level of Great Completion. These practices focus on the empty aspect of reality, which is called "alpha purity", literally, meaning that it is pure from the beginning. This is one of the many, unique terms of Great Completion. Unfortunately, it is often mis-translated as "primordial purity" which is another term often used in Mahamudra and with a very different feeling and sense to it. Alpha purity is accessed through the Thorough Cut. Again, that has been poorly translated as "cutting through" which is not what the term means. Then, the emptiness has to be filled in with enlightenment. In Great Completion, that is done using the Direct Crossing practice. In this practice, the liveliness of the emptiness is gradually developed and then finally exhausted through a sequence of four sets of appearances. Again, these have been mistranslated as "visions". This is a complicated subject and cannot be explained here but, succinctly stated, these are not "visions" by any means; they are sets of appearances that occur to mind.

When these two practices are unified, the result is the final attainment of the Great Completion path, which is that one's body dissipates into light, which is in rainbow colours. In short, this is making a prayer for blessings so that the whole path of innermost Great Completion can be successfully traversed.

The evil deeds and obscurations of body of my
successive lives without exception are purified
Bless me to attain the migrator-taming
nirmanakaya.

From a red ĀḤ at the throat of the glorious guru
Red light radiating in chains
Enters the red bindu at my throat and
That bindu becomes vividly marked with an ĀḤ
letter.
The evil deeds and obscurations of speech of my
successive lives without exception are purified
Bless me to attain the stoppageless sambhogakaya.

From an azure blue HŪṂ at the heart of the
glorious guru
Azure blue light radiating in chains
Enters the azure blue bindu at my heart and
That bindu becomes vividly marked with a HŪṂ
letter.
The evil deeds and obscurations of mind of my
successive lives without exception are purified
Grant your blessings that I attain the birthless
dharmakaya.

From a red HRĪḤ at the navel of the glorious guru
Five types of light radiating in chains
Enter the red bindu at my navel and
That bindu becomes vividly marked with an HRĪḤ
letter.
The evil deeds and obscurations of my three doors
equally without exception are purified

Grant your blessings that I attain the
svabhavikakaya.

Finally, through intense longing devotion
The guru with consort melts into a ball of light
And we merge as one inseparable in the experienced
expanse of rigpa.
Inexpressible by speech and thought,
Samantabhadra's enlightened mind expanse, A."

With that, your mind and the guru's mind suddenly mingle inseparably and, after that, you stay in it. When movement occurs, look directly at its entity.

Third, the technique for looking at mind further has both seeking shamatha[17] through reliance on conceptual tokens and preserving shamatha through reliance on absence of conceptual tokens[18].

---

[17] Tib. zhi gnas. Literally, calm-abiding. Shamatha itself is the ability to put your mind on anything and have it stay there one-pointedly, without distraction, for as long as you desire. The practices involved in "finding" meaning "getting to" that state are also often called "shamatha" for short.

[18] See the glossary.

First, place a small item[19] before you then look at it one-pointedly with undistracted eye and awareness[20]. If you go off into non-abiding, look by mixing the discursive thought and the eye with the small item. Rest just by doing short sessions. If you follow those instructions but a strong experience of abiding does not occur, look many times in short sessions. At the end of that, visualize an azure blue HŪṂ letter at your heart centre. From it, many HŪṂ letters come forth in a uninterrupted stream and wind in a clockwise direction around the small item from before until a HŪṂ sits atop the small item, and that is how you focus your rigpa. Then, continue the meditation with the HŪṂ's gradually returning and dissolving back into the HŪṂ at the heart centre. Again, rest. Meditation here is just familiarizing your mind with that. Then, your body turns into a blue HŪṂ letter, and, just not touching the ground, you send it off in progressively through the roads and mountain sides. Rest just by being non-forgetful. Again, as before, return it back. Meditate like that many times. At the end of that, meditate on this: there is one HŪṂ each at your heart centre and one before you; from the HŪṂ of the heart centre, one HŪṂ comes out and strikes the HŪṂ before you; that HŪṂ blazes into greater brilliance, enters the Brahmā aperture and dissolves into the HŪṂ of the heart centre. Meditate on that until you finalize it. That will assist abiding a little. This is shamatha with conceptual tokens.

---

[19] Tib. rde'u. The term means a little thing, like a small pebble or stone or anything else at all that you can fix your gaze, and mind with it, upon.

[20] Tib. shes pa. Awareness here means the basic consciousness of the senses, in this case both eye and mind.

Second, preserving shamatha without conceptual tokens. With the key points of body and the gaze as before, meditate on the endlessly kind guru at the crown, supplicate him one-pointedly, and he dissolves into you after which, when you set yourself gently in rigpa, you go a little into an empty evenness[21]; that is abiding. From that state, discursive thought darts out here and there; that is movement. The eliminator of the movement, that is rigpa. Through practising at lengthening the time that you can stay within a continuity of that, first, discursive thought will increase in amount, and when that happens, it is "initial abiding"[22]. Through practising at uninterruptedly preserving that state, discursive thought will ease up and abiding will increase. And, the movement will improve the abiding rather than adversely affecting it. That is called "medium abiding"[23]. By continuing on at preserving its continuity like that, finally, your abiding will last for as long as you decide to abide. At that time, appearances come with a very pure bliss, a very precise clarity, and even though a little discursive thought might come along, the abiding is unaffected by it; that is called "shamatha"[24]. Medi

---

[21] Even-ness here does not refer to a quality of the abiding, rather it is experiential language, an ancient word for emptiness which actually being experienced.

[22] This really means "an initial level of shamatha" in which can abide for the first time.

[23] This means "a middling level of shamatha" in which you have developed a moderate ability to abide though it is still not full-blown shamatha.

[24] This is not shamatha as a practice but the shamatha which is the

(continued...)

tating till you obtain finalization of just that is an exceptionally important point.

When you look at its entity[25], discursive thought will shine forth[26] in a very obvious way and, by looking directly at it, an empty evenness comes and that itself is vipashyana shining forth[27]. Through practising at preserving the stream of it, the experience of bliss-clarity increases. Not being attached to it but looking at its essence is important.

Due to having merged the three of abiding, moving, and rigpa'ing[28] that go with that kind of preserving into one, even if

---

[24](...continued)
end result of the practice of the same name.

[25] Its entity means the entity of the abiding mind.

[26] Tib. 'char ba. This is a special term that refers to something coming forth in mind or the entity of mind, either one. It is not the same word as appearing because appearance implies being on the side of the object, in this system. To simply translate this term as "to appear", as is often done because it sounds better in English, is to undermine the terminology of the system in a way that makes it impossible for the English reader to make the clear distinctions that a reader of the Tibetan would immediately see.

[27] Again, note that vipashyana is not an appearance that comes to mind but is mind "shining forth", coming out, in a certain way.

[28] The noun is rigpa, which means knowing in a general way but also has connotations that do not translate into English. It is often translated these days as "awareness" but that is a major error. I therefore do not translate it. The word has both noun

(continued...)

discursive thought does move, it will be empty. I consider this to be the great level of one-pointedness[29]. In this context, you might, during the passage of sleep, dream that you fall into an abyss or have a frightening dream, in which case it[30] acts as a conditioner so that, right within the dream itself, you will able be abide at length in empty evenness until, at the end, you will sometimes want to wake up and you might think, "Is this luminosity?" In this context also, it will happen that, except for the mindfulness that is shepherding the continuity, there will be nothing at all to meditate on. Sometimes when sleeping, a light like a small, circular moon will shine forth and that can increase to the point where it is like the brilliance of the sun, illuminating the whole house. Things like the luminosity mentioned above and these other developments will manifest.

Then, planting devotion to the guru like a stake, preserve it and by doing that, the bliss-clarity experience from before

---

[28](...continued)
and verb forms, here it is the verb form. Mind can abide, move within that abiding, and there can be a knower of a very insightful type, which knows dynamically and insightfully, what is happening with the abiding and, or, movement. In other words, there is abiding, moving, and rigpa'ing.

[29] In the Mahamudra system of Shantipa, which is what the Drukpa Kagyus follow, there are not only the Four Yogas of Mahamudra, but each of those is subdivided into lesser, middling, and greater levels of accomplishment. He is referring to the peak level of accomplishment of the first yoga, the Yoga of One-pointedness.

[30] The abiding as far as you have developed it, as just described.

will once and for all become: an abiding but one that is the least common denominator, which is absent of "it is this, it is not that"; absent of grasping at abiding and not abiding, empty and not empty. You might doubt yourself; at the time of sleep the outer object and your own body can go empty and the dread from it will wake you up with a start. During the day, it will seem that, except for just being un-distracted, there is be nothing to whatsoever to do. That is the key point of keeping a steady continuity of doing the preserving.

Sometimes discursive thought might come darting out all over the place, in which case say a forceful PHAṬ and look directly at the entity[31]. Or sometimes say a particularly forceful PHAṬ and, mixing expanse and rigpa[32], aim your gaze into space; through meditating like that rigpa and outer appearances will not have a chance to separate into their individual components[33]. When you remain undistracted, there is no chance for any of the appearing objects of the eightfold group to be grasped onto with conceptual thinking that says, "It is this. It is that"; instead it will go onto a empty evenness. When you become distracted, that does not happen. At this time[34], we are mostly in distraction or forgetfulness, so to preserve the entity again and again using the shepherd of mindfulness is an important key point.

---

[31] Of the thought.

[32] Here expanse is a Vajra Vehicle practical term of emptiness.

[33] Dualistic thought will not be able to re-assert itself.

[34] Meaning now, in our unpractised, un-accomplished state ...

In this context, at the time of sleep also, sometimes a mere clarity can result in apprehending luminosity, sometimes an absence of clarity might go into an empty evenness, sometimes the clarity might appear just as itself and what is related to it, and sometimes, a dream can, in the space of rigpa, go on to self-shining-forth-self-liberation. Those various ways of shining forth are the common awareness[35] of buddha-mind, the actuality of sentient beings.

When you see dharmakaya's entity nakedly, like this, you might think, "Is this the meeting[36] with it?" Thorough Cut's actuality is realized and Direct Crossing's liveliness is trained in and through this process materiality is liberated into a mass of light; this is the approach is evident in the texts of Great Completion.

From beginning to end, the things connected with this—experiences arising or not, actuality being realized or not, obstructors and points of deviation being present or not, and so on—happen only in dependence on devotion to the guru so even for this lowly old man, there has only been supplication to the guru alone. And, it has been through planting the stake of devotion that just a little of the guru's kind realization has arisen in my mindstream. Practitioners of the future too will cherish supplicating the guru because if they do make

---

[35] Tib. tha mal gyi shes pa.

[36] Tib. ngo 'phrod pa. The intransitive form of ngo sprod pa. When somebody introduces dharmakaya to you it is the transitive form. When you have been introduced to and therefore have met with, it is the intransitive form, as mentioned here.

efforts at guru devotion, they will find that it brings them the profound key points of all instructions that exist right within that practice.

Even if you do realize the face of mind, if you do not "extract the profit", realization will not leap higher. This extraction of profit is an exceptionally important point thus, given that the supreme extractor of profit is guru devotion: meditate on the guru at your crown; supplicate like planting a stake; and meditate assiduously while his mind and yours have not merged. Through that, the profit will definitely be extracted.

Then, when any of the utterly wretched five poisons has risen, if you do not stop it, but look directly at its entity, then it will go onto empty evenness. That is wisdom. If, when you hear intolerably bad words from others such as false accusations of wrongdoing, you can liberate the poisons by looking at their entity, that will cause a great extraction of profit to occur.

When beginners are preserving the face of mind, there can be many problems with sinking, fogginess, dullness, and so on, so the method for dispelling those faults is this. If the rigpa is agitated, relax body and mind. With a squint, aim your gaze down at the edge of your mat. If you are going dull, aim the gaze into space and tighten up the rigpa a little. If you are sinking, raise the eyes up. Gently identifying each discursive thought, one at a time, as it comes with rigpa is important. Doing that will dispel the faults.

My vajra relative Chophel pressed me insistently saying, "I need a profound instruction that will benefit my mind", so, even though I have not the slightest good qualities of mind and it really is not all right for someone like myself, who is so resistant that these matters are hidden from me, to speak falsely about things I have no experience of, still, I cannot reject the petitioner so, having supplicated the refuge, endlessly kind Tenpa'i Nyima, this lowly old man Shakya Shri wrote this during the winter session by the light of a lamp.

> I think to myself, "Could this very abbreviated
> instruction given to assist with mind
> Be of benefit to a few people of inferior intelligence
> like myself?"
> If there are mistakes or contradictions in it, I lay
> them aside in Samantabhadra's expanse.
> May the virtue of it ripen and liberate all migrators.

Eka praticcha'o.

ཨོཾ༔ FROM THE KINGLY PEAK OF THE VEHICLES, ATI GREAT COMPLETION: THOROUGH CUT'S SECRET PATH, THE SECOND CORE PIECE, INSTRUCTION ON NAKEDLY SEEING RIGPA

by Drubwang Shakya Shri

ཨོཾ༔ I pay homage to and take refuge in the primordial protector, Guru Great Bliss's body[37].

In the very secret[38] anthology of Accomplishing Guru Great Bliss, the stages of the path of the secret[39] has the two sections of alpha purity Thorough Cut and spontaneous existence

---

[37] The name Guru Great Bliss refers to the name of a treasure revealed by Shakya Shri. However, there is a play on words here. The great bliss body is the fourth kāya, which is the fact of great bliss experienced when the three kāyas are complete and functioning together. Therefore, he is not taking refuge in the body meaning the bodily form of Guru Great Bliss but taken refuge in the body of enlightenment as a whole of Guru Great Bliss.

[38] Tib. yang sang. "Very secret" here is specifically the name of one of the several types of revealed treasure.

[39] The secret means the Vajra Vehicle teaching.

Direct Crossing. Of them, the Thorough Cut instruction is the subject of this text.

The instruction has three parts: the preliminary part, which is research into the three arising, abiding, and going; the main part, which arrival at alpha purity's rigpa; and the conclusion, which is how the rigpa, the alpha purity's liveliness, is completed.

1. The Preliminary Part

To begin with, at the start of a session, guru yoga is done as follows. From the expanse of your three doors divorced from elaborations, self-appearance, stoppageless liveliness, self-knowing wisdom's dakini comes in a body white with red lustre[40]. With mood warm and smiling her hair hangs down loosed, and her right hand sounds a chang te'u of the secret[41] in space. Her left hand holds a skull-cup filled with fluid of un-outflowed amrita at her heart centre. She is draped with bone five symbolic ornaments and her bhaga and breasts are exceptionally full. She dances on a seat of lotus and moon. In the space above and before her, on the seat of a moon disk spread across a one-hundred thousand petal lotus, the summation of all refuges in person, the entity in the form of the guru, Guru Great Bliss with a white body adorned with many

---

[40] A white body with a lustre of red on the highlights of the body, as is often seen in paintings of white deities. The two colours symbolize emptiness and compassion respectively.

[41] Again, the secret is the path of Vajra Vehicle, which is secret or hidden compared to the conventional vehicle of sutra.

marks and illustrative signs, extremely peaceful and smiling looks into the expanse of space with round[42] eyes. He wears the lotus hat on his head and on his body the layers of the white secret robe, the dark blue phoka, and the dharma robes with golden patra design. On top of his two hands in equipoise mudra, he holds a skullcup filled with fluid of deathless amrita. His feet are crossed evenly and, within a space in which chains of light ropes of rainbow light bindus are intermeshing, he sits obviously full of joy. Supplicate him one-pointedly. Then, with your body hairs standing on end and tears flowing, with your speech crying out "Oh" with intense longing and supplicating with the pleasant melody of drawing the horse along, and with a mind of intense, unbearable devotion in a state not departing from seeing the guru as actual buddha, recite whatever supplications are suitable. At the end of that, the guru turns into a ball of light then dissolves into you.

Refresh yourself in the state of your three doors and the guru's enlightened body, speech, and mind being inseparable, remaining equipoised on that for a little while. If, within that state, discursive thought suddenly arises, look into its initial place of arising. For the class of things[43], carefully investigate where it arises from: your skandhas, dhatus, and ayatanas; the inanimate container worlds; the animate sentient beings contained in them, and so on. If you do not discover a place

[42] Round in these contexts means wide open, staring wide, as opposed to looking with a squint.

[43] Things here means the things that a conceptual mind believes to be things.

of arising in the class of things, carefully examine where it arises from among non-things: empty space, that is, above, below, the cardinal directions, and so on. In the interim, where is its place of abiding? Does it abide in your skandhas, dhatus, ayatanas in the six forms of outer flesh, the internal flesh, the nine orifices, the tip of the head with its orifices to the tips of the feet, and so on? If it abides there, then analyse carefully to see exactly how it does abide. At the end, which place does it go to? Does it go to the external objects of the sixfold group[44], the five doors of the sense faculties, and so on? Analyse exactly how it does go and, for as long as you do not come to a firm decision, keep honing in on it assiduously.

In the interim[45], is this mind of yours—the one that becomes a buddha, the one that falls into the bad migrations, the one that has the feelings of good and bad—is it present as a thing or a non-thing? If it is present as a thing, carefully investigate to see what kind characteristics—form, colour, shape—it is present with. If you think that it is a non-thing, then, since it is empty space with the basis of not being perceptible, carefully investigate how just how this one that experiences is present—mind happy or unhappy, mind cold or hungry or thirsty these three, and so on. At the end, are the pair of perceptions of object analysed and the analyser one thing or different things? If you think, "They are one", then what kind of characteristics is it present with? If they are present

---

[44] The sixfold group is the set of six consciousnesses which we as humans have.

[45] Talking about the interim phase when it is present as something.

as separate things, then the three of arising, abiding, and going have separated off to one side and the analyzer has separated off to another side and the two appear individually. Nonetheless, until you come to a firm mental[46] decision that that appearing item is without the distinctions of exists and does not exist, and so on in the expanse of mindness[47] alone, you should assiduously hone in on it and make efforts to come to a firm decision.

The non-discovery of an initial place of arising brings the birthless essence empty, dharmakaya. The non-discovery of an interim place of abiding brings the stoppageless nature luminosity, sambhogakaya. The non-discovery of a place of going at the end brings non-abiding compassionate activity nirmanakaya. Rest up a little in that state of self-introduction to the three kayas. Then, stay in the state of equipoise in the state without even a speck of meditation to be done, in which there is no analysis that recycles events of the past, no going to greet a future that lies ahead, no activity of rational mind in the present that would think, "This present moment is empty", no creation of good discursive thoughts, no stopping

---

[46] Here, mental means rational mind. He is not talking about gaining realization of it but just come to a clear certainty that that is how it is.

[47] Tib. sems nyid. "Mindness" is a path term for the essence of mind. It is a specific term of the higher tantras which does not mean "the very mind" as has often been translated, where mind is the dualistic mind of samsara, but what mind really is, which is also called the essence or entity of mind. Mind is the samsaric version and mindness is the nirvanic version that underlies the complex apparatus of samsaric mind.

of bad ones, a state in which every appearance that shines forth in whichever way self-appears-self-liberates unmodified and unspoiled by an antidote, and you are settled into just being what it is; that is the holy type of abiding.

That completes the first practice of training the mind.

2. The Main Part

When the ordinary training of mind has been done to the point that a greater degree of certainty in the practice has been attained, there is the main part, the extraordinary alpha purity Thorough Cut instruction, which is done as a determination of the key points of nakedly seeing rigpa.

On the side of the fiction's concepts, to start with, assiduously supplicate the kind root guru who you visualize seated at your crown, on a lotus and moon. The guru, who melts into light, and you merge inseparable. Then from the experienced space of superfactual[48] rigpa which is the empty-luminous character[49], discursive thinking that thinks, "It is the guru" is an item there in its own place within that self-empty character; this merging of enlightened mind and mind[50] into one is

---

[48] See the glossary.

[49] Here character means your innate character, your actual disposition.

[50] That is to say, the result of your samsaric mentality with the enlightened mind of the guru. This started as part of fictional truth in the supplication phase and moved to superfactual truth

(continued...)

the profound key point of the completion of the great liveliness of rigpa[51]. ITHI ཨིཐི[52]

Unchanging body which is the underpinning of Mountain Chog Zhag[53] is as follows. The body is put into a posture having the Seven Dharmas of Vairochana or a posture coming from mindness set into relaxation—as you like—and, separated from all movement as though it had become Mt. Meru, just sit there staying in how it is[54].

---

[50](...continued)
when the merging was complete. The result is that you experience not only the empty part of rigpa but its liveliness as part of that emptiness. That is the great point of the practice of rigpa in which the liveliness of the rigpa is fully part of the rigpa.

[51] The fact that a thought can arise and be part of that innate character is the profound key point of the Thorough Cut practice in which there is not only the empty aspect of the rigpa which most practitioners first experience but the liveliness of the rigpa complete with it. That is not merely the liveliness of the rigpa but the liveliness of rigpa together with the emptiness, which is the culmination and completion of Thorough Cut practice.

[52] ITHI is a mark of the secret mantra system which indicates that this is a profound secret not to be passed on lightly.

[53] Thorough Cut teaching includes a teaching on the four Chog Zhag. This term has no easy translation. It means something like "just being there as it is".

[54] Tib. rang babs su chog ger sdod. Stay in this Chog Zhag, in whatever is just as it is because of the non-movement.

Not moving the eyes to and fro, the Ocean Chog Zhag, is used to focus singlemindedly on the task as follows. Not engaging at all in any consciously produced activity of speech, such talking, reciting mantra, adjusting the winds, and so on, and with the mouth left so that the teeth are just not touching and the wind of the breath made very gentle, you train in absence of consciously produced activity. Then your eyes, very round and without any movement at all, are put, like planting a spear, up into empty space.

Rigpa—which is beyond mind[55]—Chog Zhag is used to arrive at a determination as follows. That mind which is not rigpa[56] in brief, is this very distraction and confusion run amok[57]. The assemblage of concepts that constitutes the mental

---

[55] Rigpa which is the mindness beyond the complex apparatus of mind that arises upon engaging in samsara …

[56] The text here says mind which is not rigpa. We have the problem that "not rigpa" has been translated as "ignorance". In most translations then, you would get "ignorant mind" but that totally fails to make the connection between rigpa and mind, the latter of which is not rigpa. There is rigpa, the point of the practice and there is the mind of samsara which is not merely the opposite of that rigpa but is a case of not rigpa'ing.

Furthermore, he just said, "rigpa—which is beyond mind". So, now he is saying, "Well, what is that mind which is not rigpa (which is the fundamental ignorance as we usually call it)?" It is like this …

[57] That you are now involved with, as a samsaric being …

events[58] are these[59] discursive thoughts involved in analyzing the past gone before, going out to greet the future, and thinking in the present, "It is this. It is not this", which are like dust motes in sun light. The primordial, original awareness[60], the self-knowing rigpa which is beyond the mind that is not rigpa, is not contaminated, not spoiled by anything at all of the three of sinking, fogginess, and dullness, or of the experiences of bliss, clarity, and no-thought, or of certainty[61], and so on. It is a state of being empty and luminous without grasping involved, so is the direct experience of transparency[62] of everything, outside and inside. In this state which is beyond being an object of verbal expression, you cross over

---

[58] When discussing samsaric consciousness, it is defined as two-fold: the primary mind which he has just defined and the assemblage of mental events that are the satellites, as they are described, of that primary mind.

[59] Meaning the ones you have going on for you now.

[60] It is common for rigpa to be translated as "awareness" which is a gross mistake. Here awareness is used correctly, as the translation of "shes pa" which refers to any consciousness in general, whether as part of rigpa or part of mind which is not rigpa.

[61] Tib. nges shes. Certainty is a specific item in samsaric mind, that is, mind which is ignorant and not rigpa. It is something to be developed on the path and is similar to the three obstacles to shamatha and the three positive experiences of meditation just mentioned in being so. In other words, rigpa is beyond all the stuff of mind that you use on the conventional path of meditation.

[62] See the glossary.

via a mindfulness without the efforts of consciousness[63] activity into the exhaustion of dharmas[64].

For the door of shining forth of the liveliness[65], no matter how it shines forth as the assemblage of concepts—whether as the five poisons, three poisons, etcetera in the context of object and subject of the sixfold group[66], because of meditating in the experienced expanse of alpha purity's view without conscious activities, it shines forth as the nature[67] and, due to

---

[63] Meaning a mindfulness which is different from the one that most people think of, one that does not have the conscious efforts and activities of dualistic mind associated with it.

[64] So far he is talking about the empty side, the side in which dualistic grasping as dharmas has been exhausted. You stay in that experience with a mindfulness that belongs to that state rather than one that belongs to this side of the pass, mindfulness that belongs to dualistic mind.

[65] Now he has moved on and is talking about the appearing aspect of the rigpa. Door of shining forth is a technical term of Great Completion that means the ways in which appearance comes forth from the alpha purity of the rigpa.

[66] Perceiver and perceived of the sixfold group of human consciousness ...

[67] This would usually be translated as "shines forth naturally" but that is not at all the meaning. It shines forth as the nature means that it shines forth as part of the innate disposition, as a feature of the mindness, as the liveliness of the rigpa, all of which are ways of saying that is shines forth as your true nature. This usage of nature is exactly that involved in the name "Nature Great Com-

(continued...)

having been liberated in that nature, there is no division into the entity and its liveliness into two, none whatsoever of the fabrication done by rational mind or mental analysis, and so on. Equally, there is neither development of good concepts of the three kayas nor abandonment of bad concepts of the five poisons. It is to practice captained by rigpa alone, captained by rigpa without conscious activities involved, beyond every extreme produced by conscious activity.

When a greater level of steadiness in that has been attained, the body, in a state without conscious activity, is kept with a straight spine. The eyes, round, are speared into the circle of space ahead. The speech, for the purpose of absence of conscious activity, together with grasping, is left how it is. Rigpa is to set yourself right within expanse and rigpa inseparable that is divorced of the three of birth, cessation, and dwelling, the great pervasive spread, without creating any limits, without falling into any sides and stay just there using the unmanufactured authentic[68] situation's mindfulness. Thereby, in that state, no matter how the liveliness's door of shining forth does shine forth, empty discursive thoughts are what will shine forth as objects whose entity is empty luminosity. In short, due to emptiness having dissolved into

---

[67](...continued)
pletion". Again, that term is usually translated as "Natural Great Completion" and that again is incorrect. Great Completion is about your nature, which is the luminosity aspect of the essence of your mind, and that specifically is why Great Completion is called "Nature, Great Completion".

[68] Authentic here is another term for reality.

emptiness, the distinctions made between shining forth and liberation have gone onto simultaneous occurrence, whereby apparent existence, which is all the dharmas of samsara and nirvana, has crossed over into the exhaustion of dharmas that is Thorough Cut's alpha purity that has no hope and fear, no creation and elimination whatsoever.

Third, there is the way that the subsequent fruition will been determined. In short, all dharmas—which are included within both externally appearing objects to the whole extent of existence including self and others, container and contents, samsara and nirvana, and the internal grasping of mindness that comes as mind which is not rigpa and as mental events' conceptual tokens with hope and fear and the antidotes coarse and subtle that go with elimination and creation—have become alpha purity and have been exhausted into dharmata, Great Completion's experienced space. Due to that, both the cause, what makes them shine forth, and the object, the place where they shine forth, have developed a simultaneous front, like a drawing made in the sky and so the perceptions of rational mind regarding past, present, and future have, all of them, sunk into rigpa, alpha purity's expanse. There are the perceptions of what has gone by in which one thinks that the going and staying, actions and behaviour, of this round light, the vivid appearances of today which follows last night and its prior daytime are "Like this". There are the perceptions of the future in which one thinks that the lump-like sleeping of the coming evening's appearances of increasing darkness will be "like this". Every one of these perceptions belonging to the rational mind's grasping that thinks, "It is like this", in relation to the lack of distinction between night and day, the place that is the destination and the person who goes there, one's dwelling which is the parent's homeland, and so on, has dissolved into alpha purity's inexpressible expanse and due to that there is not recognizing[69] and that which is beyond object of rational mind. Here, the three factors of the preserving mindfulness—with conscious effort, without conscious effort, and so on—and the entity to be preserved and the self-liveliness have equally been purified. Thus it is luminous while it is being empty, empty while being clarity and in that unshifting state right over the innate character that is without the time of the three times, the empty clarity having a core of rigpa, the daytime perceptions of self and the nighttime dreams of confusion have gone into simultaneous purification of the luminosity of unconfused experience. The distinctions of resting and not resting are not recognized and mind has gone on display as that beyond rational mind, the transparency of inseparable expanse and rigpa; just this is the fruition of alpha purity Thorough Cut having been determined.

The best yogin, the one who goes to the end of the practice like that, leaving behind the impure portion of just hair and nails, lets the pure portion of the body dissipate into atoms. In the internalized luminosity of rigpa's primordial expanse, in the experienced space of the enclosure of the youthful vase body, ground appearances have dissolved into rigpa, which is buddhahood as the dharmakaya. Once again, from alpha purity, the primordial expanse, the two types of spontaneous existence's form kayas arise without conscious effort and, in each moment, each of tens of hundreds of thousands of

---

[69] Where recognition is a process of rational mind.

millions of emanations for the sake of migrators are sent off and shake out the deep pit of samsara.

The one of medium level faculty has a mode of buddhahood exemplified by sun and moon rising and setting. Just like the moon appears in conjunction with the passage of the sun on the fifteenth lunar day, the seal of the yogin's body collapses and at the same time he dissolves into alpha purity, the primordial expanse. Then, in each instant, countless numbers of emanations shake the deep pit of samsara out.

The one of least level of faculty has a mode of liberation in the first bardo as follows. Like a snake shedding its skin, this person, having been struck by a fatal illness, goes progressively through the stages of dissolution of earth, water, fire, and wind to the point where his outer breath stops and then through the dissolutions of flaring of appearance and end of flaring to the point where his inner breath stops. Then, the ground luminosity, which is like a mother, and the luminosity that is the experience come from his practice, which is like a son, dissolve inseparably and then, having become buddha again, emanations for the sake of migrators are produced, without effort of conscious activity, as spontaneous existence.

There is one of even lower level of faculty who has a mode of liberation at the end of the bardo like a child leaping into its mother's lap. Like a child coming together with its mother without needing to check on whether this is its mother or not, the spontaneous existence bardo's three of sounds, lights, and rays, and its bindus with small bindus of peaceful and wrathful kayas no matter how they shine forth, are rigpa's self-liveliness and, while recognized, there is trust, and, finally, having dissolved into those very kayas, complete buddhahood is manifest right there.

Then there are those of exceptionally dull faculty. Persons who obtain the ripening empowerments and liberating instructions of Great Completion then have perseverance that is focussed to the exclusion of all else, even if they are the most ordinary of persons who have not let go of the three—outer, inner, and secret—samayas in relation to guru and dharma, will, because this is concerned with the blessings of guru and lineage and the infallible liberation on seeing the dharma of Great Completion, have the door of birth to the six families and bad migrations cut and will then have a miraculous birth from within the bud of a lotus flower in one of the five fields of emanations which are like optical illusions. Having done so, they will see the face and hear the speech of buddha and then, having entered the bodhisatva's vehicle, will have every one of the obscurations to knowledge purified by degrees and then will attain buddhahood.

Briefly, all dispelling of obstacles and taking of profit comes about due to devotion and supplication to the guru. Thus, keeping the guru in mind, remembering him, and thinking that there is nothing except for him, with eyes always wet from tears pouring down, at all times and in all circumstances persevere at supplicating him.

What was said above came on the arms of the snow mountain Lofty Blue Queen, in 7Jetsun Rinpoche's[70] practice place Crystal Cave Plaintain Tree Fortress. There, through 7Orgyen Rinpoche's blessings, coming from the casket of expanse-rigpa spread everywhere, it was determined and expressed by Pawo Rigtsal Thogmey[71]. I wrote this based on the signs[72] that shone forth from the indivisible expanse-rigpa, ornamenting it a little with my own experience so it will not be the domain of anyone except for five, perhaps seven fortunate ones with sharp faculties, and therefore it is sealed with an exceptionally tight command-seal. ITHI ཨྠི. The command contained here is entrusted to the protectress of mantra, Ekajati, and to Remati, so guard it! Do not let it slip into the hands of those without the samaya. Guhya. Sign dissolved. It was written down by Padma Chogdrup.

---

[70] The 7 here and just beyond is not a mistake. In Tibetan literature, there are several ways to honour a person's name when it is written. One very honorific way is to place the numeral seven before the person's name. The numeral seven indicates that this is a person who possesses what the Buddha called "the seven riches of the noble ones". They are a set of seven very fine qualities belonging to beings who have trained themselves well spiritually.

[71] Shakya Shri's treasure revealer name.

[72] Means the symbols that communicated the meaning.

GLOSSARY

Actuality, Tib. gnas lugs: A key term in the Vajra Vehicle in general. It is one of a pair of terms, the other being snang lugs. This term means how any given situation actually is and its counterpart means how something appears. In short, something could appear in many different ways, depending on the circumstances at the time and on the being perceiving it. However, regardless of circumstances, it will always have its own actuality, its own situation of how it really is. You could also think of this pair of terms as meaning "a thing's reality and its surface appearance". Note that this term also gets special use in Great Completion. In that case there is less sense of it being part of the pair and a much stronger sense of it talking about a reality that is present and which actually is that way.

Adventitious, Tib. glo bur: Often translated as "sudden", the word "adventitious" in English more accurately reflects the full meaning of the original Tibetan. Something adventitious is something which suddenly comes up as a surface event and disappears again in regard to something else since it does not belong to the core of the thing that it appeared on the surface of.

Alpha purity, Tib. ka dag: a unique Great Completion term meaning purity that is there from the first, that is, primordial purity. There are many general terms that express the notion of "primordial purity" but this one is unique and stands out. Some people do not like the term "alpha purity" but, funnily enough, this is exactly what the Tibetan says.

Alteration, altered, same as contrivance q.v.

Bliss, clarity, and no-thought, Tib. bde gsal mi rtog pa: mentioned in this text as three temporary experiences that practitioners invariably meet in meditation. Bliss is ease of the body and-or mind, clarity is the experience of extraordinary clarity of mind, and no-thought is the experience literally of no thoughts happening in the mind. There is another understanding of these three not as temporary experiences to be eschewed but final experiences of realization.

Chog Zhag, Tib. cog bzhag: There are four chog zhag. They are a part of the Thorough Cut teaching of Great Completion. They are four ways of resting so that you are chog zhag "being just so". The four way of being just so correspond to view, meditation, conduct, and fruition of the Thorough Cut practice. Essentially, the teaching of the four "being just so's", can both introduce the idea of what Thorough Cut is about and equally be used to give profound instruction on the whole of Thorough Cut.

Clarity, Tib. gsal ba: when you see this term, it should be understood as an abbreviation of the full term in Tibetan, 'od gsal ba, which is usually translated as luminosity. It is not another factor of mind distinct from luminosity but merely a convenient abbreviation in both Indian and Tibetan dharma language for the longer term, luminosity. See "Luminosity" in this glossary for more.

Common Mind, Tib. tha mal gyi shes pa: the path term used in the Mahāmudrā tradition to indicate mind's essence. In Dzogchen, the equivalent term is “rigpa”. Both words are used by practitioners as a sort of code word for their own, personal experience of the essence of mind. These words are secret because of the power they are connected and should be kept that way.

Tha mal gyi shaypa is often referred to as “ordinary mind”, a term that was established by Chogyam Trungpa Rinpoche for his students. However, there are two problems with that word. Firstly, “tha mal” does not mean “ordinary”. It means “common”, something that is common to everyone. This is well attested to in the writings of the Kagyu forefathers. Secondly, this is not mind, given that mind is used throughout this book to mean the dualistic mind of beings in cyclic existence. Rather this is “shes pa”, the most general term for all kinds of awareness or knower. In short, it is the kind of non-dualistic knower that is common to everyone.

From a practitioner’s perspective, there is little difference between the two terms. However, as Tsoknyi Rinpoche points out,There is a deep point concerning what is explained in the extraordinary levels of Dzogchen as the complexion aspect of the rigpa[1] and what is explained in Mahāmudrā as the luminosity aspect[2]. Dzogchen says that real rigpa is to bring forth the deep state which is the luminosity part without the slightest bit of compartmentalizing—the actual original, naked dharmakāya—and there is a slight point of discussion over that.

“There is that sort of discussion when these things are being explained but, from the perspective of an individual receiving the instructions and meditating, the instructions on Mahāmudrā could become the accomplishment of Dzogchen and vice-versa. That difference is explained in the texts but in fact it depends on the individual.””

Conceptual Tokens, Tib. mtshan ma. Conceptual tokens are the structures of conceptual mind that conceptual mind uses for perception. For example, you could see a table in direct visual perception of table or you could think "table" in a conceptual perception of table. In the latter case, there is a conceptual structure or token that is the label "table" used by conceptual mind when it thinks table.

Confusion, Tib. 'khrul pa: the Tibetan term means fundamental delusion's confusion of taking things the wrong way. This is not the other meaning in English of having lots of thoughts and being confused about it. It is much more fundamental than that. The definition in Tibetan is "confusion is the appearance to rational mind of something being present when it is not" and refers for example to seeing any object, such as a table, as being truly present when in fact it is present only as mere appearance which has occurred in a process of interdependent arising.

Contrivance, contrived, Tib. bcos pa: something which has been altered from its native state or the process of making that alteration.

Cyclic existence, Skt. saṃsāra, Tib. 'khor ba: the type of existence that sentient beings have which is that they continue on from one existence to another, always within the enclosure of births that are produced by ignorance and experienced as unsatisfactory.

Dharmakaya, Tib. chos sku: the mind aspect of a buddha which, in the Thorough Cut system, is the fruition level of the direct perception of the essence of mind.

Dharmata, Tib. chos nyid: Dharmatā means any given sphere of realities. There is not one dharmatā of reality as has been thought amongst Western translators till now but as many dharmatā's as one cares to speak of. For example, even the fact of water's wetness can be referred to as the dharmatā of water, meaning how it actually is. The term is very similar to actuality but refers to a whole sphere taken as a single reality whereas actuality refers to the specific reality of any given reality.

Direct Crossing, Tib. tho rgal: one of the two practices of the innermost level of Great Completion practice. The other is Thorough Cut.

Discursive thought, Tib. rnam rtog: this means more than just the superficial thought that is heard as a voice in the head. It includes the entirety of conceptual process that arises due to mind contacting any object of any of the senses. Discursive thought here translates from the Sanskrit original where the meaning is "conceptual thought that arises from the mind wandering among the various superficies perceived in the doors of the senses".

Effort, Tib. rtsol ba: This term in Tibetan does not merely mean effort but has the specific connotation of effort of dualistic mind. It is effort that is produced by and functions specifically within the context of dualistic concept. For example mindfulness with effort specifically means "a type of mindfulness that is occurring within the context of dualistic mind and its various operations".

Elaboration, Tib. spro ba: to be producing thoughts.

Enlightenment Mind, Skt. bodhicitta, Tib. byang chub sems: A key term of the Great Vehicle. The term refers to the mind connected with the enlightenment of a truly complete buddha (as opposed to an arhat). As such, it is a mind that is concerned with bringing all sentient beings to that same level of buddhahood. It refers both to the mind of a person on the path and to the mind of a buddha who has completed the path, therefore it is not "mind striving for enlightenment" as is so often translated but enlightenment mind, that kind of mind which is connected with the full enlightenment of a truly complete buddha. The term is used in the conventional Great Vehicle and also in the Vajra Vehicle. When Tsoknyi Rinpoche uses the term in this book, he is mainly talking about it in relation to the Vajra Vehicle understanding of the term which is a less dualistic understanding than the one of the conventional Great Vehicle.

Entity, Tib. ngo bo: see under Essence in this glossary.

Equipoise and post-attainment, Tib. mnyam bzhag and rjes thob: often mis-translated as meditation and post-meditation, "equipoise and post-attainment" is a correct rendering. There is great meaning in the words and that meaning is lost by the looser translation. Note that equipoise and post-attainment are used throughout the three vehicles and that they have a very different meaning in Great Completion than in lower vehicles.

Essence, Tib. ngo bo: a key term used throughout Buddhist theory. The original in Sanskrit and the term in Tibetan, too, has both meanings of "essence" and "entity". In some situations the term has more the first meaning and in others, the second. For example, when speaking of mind and mind's essence, it is referring to the core or essential part within mind. On the other hand, when speaking of fire or some other thing, there is the entity, fire, and so on, and its characteristics, such as heat, and so on; in this case, it is not an essence but an entity.

Expanse, Skt. dhātu, Tib. dbyings: A Sanskrit term with over twenty meanings in Sanskrit and many of those meanings also in the Tibetan. In this book, it is used in one specific sense of the Vajra Vehicle teachings where it is the practical term for the experience of emptiness. In this sense, it means a whole "range" the whole extent of possible experience because that entire extent is covered by emptiness. Where emptiness is a very dry term, this term gives the sense of the full extent of experience that is known as the basic space within which all phenomena appear.

Fictional Truth, Tib. kun rdzob bden pa: one of a pair of terms; the other is Superfactual Truth, q.v. The usual translation as "relative truth" is not the meaning at all of this key term. The term means the level of reality (*truth*) made up by the obscuration of an ordinary person's mind. Because this is an obscured version of actual truth it is *fictional*. However, it is true for the beings who make it up, so it is still called *truth*.

Foremost Instructions, Skt. upadeśha, Tib. man ngag: there are several types of instruction mentioned in Buddhist literature: there is the general level of instruction which is the meaning contained in the words of the texts of the tradition; on a more personal and direct level there is oral instruction which has been passed down from teacher to student from the time of the buddha; and on the most profound level there is upadesha which are oral instructions provided by one's guru which are the core instructions that come out of personal experience and which convey the teaching concisely and with the full weight of personal experience. Upadesha are crucial to the vajrayāna path because these are the special way of passing on the profound instructions needed for the student's realization.

Ground, Tib. gzhi: the first member of the formulation of ground, path, and fruition. Ground, path, and fruition is the way that the teachings of the path of oral instruction belonging to the Vajra Vehicle are presented to students. Ground refers to the basic situation as it is.

Introduction and To Introduce; Tib. ngos sprad and ngos sprod pa respectively: This pair of terms is usually translated in the U.S.A. these days as "pointing out" "and "to point out" but this is yet another common mistake that has become, unfortunately, entrenched. The terms are the standard terms used in day to day life for the situation in which one person introduces another person to someone or something. They are the exact same words as our English "introduction" and "to introduce". In the Vajra Vehicle, these terms are specifically used for the situation in which one person introduces another to the nature of the person's own mind. As a matter of interest, there is another term in Tibetan for "pointing out". That term is never used for the purpose here because here, no-one points out anything. Rather, a person is introduced by another to a part of that person that he has forgotten about. There is a further problem here which is that, if "pointing out" is used for this term, when the actual Tibetan term for "pointing out" is used, there will be confusion over the terms.

Key points, Tib. gnad: it is not apparent from the wording but a "key point" is not a point of understanding that you have conceptually in your mind and take to meditation practice but is an issue belonging to the actual process of meditation itself. Meditation as a process has key points or issues within it and instructions such as the "Three Lines" are given so that the practitioner can connect a correct understanding which is derived from those instructions with those issues as they are actually present in the meditation itself. This is worth thinking over because the common understanding in English of "key point" is an instruction to be applied but that is quite incorrect; the instructions are applied to your meditation in order to work the key points that are present as issues in the meditation itself. They are the buttons existing in the meditation for you to press using the instructions that allow you to hit the buttons.

Liveliness, Tib. rtsal: another key term in Mahāmudrā and Great Completion. The term means the potential that something contains for it to produce or display some kind of expression. For example, a baby horse has the innate ability that will later come out as its liveliness of galloping and prancing as a steed. However, the term also is used in situations where the energy is actually happening, that is, it is not mere potential any more but is the energy at the time of its expression. The term that seems to fit correctly in English is "spunk", unfortunately not many people know this word well. It is the potential and the expression of dynamic display that something has within it.

Luminosity, Skt. prabhāsvara, Tib. 'od gsal ba: the core of mind, called mind's essence, has two aspects, parts, or factors as they are called. One is emptiness and the other is knowing. Luminosity is a metaphor for the fundamental knowing quality of the essence of mind. It is sometimes translated as "clear light" but that is a mistake that comes from not understanding how the words of the Tibetan go together. It does not refer to a light that is clear but refers to the illuminative property which is the hallmark of mind. Mind knows, that is what it does. Thus, it has the property of luminosity which knows its own content. Both in Sanskrit and Tibetan Buddhist literature, the term is frequently abbreviated just to gsal ba, "clarity", with the same meaning.

Mind, Skt. chitta, Tib. sems: the process of mind which occurs because there is ignorance. Mind is a saṃsāric phenomenon. It is equivalent to "dualistic mind".

Mindness, Skt. chittata, Tib. sems nyid. Mindness is a specific term of the tantras. It is one of many terms meaning the essence of mind or the nature of mind. It conveys the sense of "what mind is at its very core". It has sometimes been translated as "mind itself" but that is a misunderstanding of the Tibetan word "nyid". The term does not mean "that thing mind" where mind refers to dualistic mind. Rather, it means the very core of dualistic mind, what mind is at root, without all of the dualistic baggage. Mindness is a path term. It refers to exactly the same thing as "actuality" or "actuality of mind" which is a ground term but does so from the practitioner's perspective. It conveys the sense to a practitioner that he might still have baggage of dualistic mind that has not been purified yet but there is a core to that mind that he can work with.

Mindfulness, Tib. dran pa: the ability to keep mind on an object of the senses. With alertness, it is one of the two causes of developing śhamatha.

Not stopped, Tib. ma 'gags pa: an important path term in both Mahāmudrā and Great Completion systems. The essence of mind has two parts: emptiness and luminosity. Both of these must come unified. However, when the practitioner does the practice, they will fall into one extreme or the other. This falling into one or the other is called "stoppage". The aim of the practice is to get to the stage in which there is both emptiness and luminosity together. In that case, there is no stoppage of falling into one extreme or the other. Thus non-stopped luminosity is a term that indicates that there is the luminosity with all of its appearance yet that luminosity, for the practitioner, is not mistaken, is not stopped off. Stopped luminosity is an experience like luminosity but in which the appearances have, at least to some extent, not been mixed with emptiness. The practitioner in that case has "alighted on", stopped off at, the appearances and become caught, at least to some extent, in them.

Outflow, Skt. sasrava, Tib. zag pa: outflows occur when wisdom loses its footing and falls into the elaborations of dualistic mind. Anything that is dualization has an outflow with it. This is sometimes translated as "defiled" or "conditioned" but these fail to capture the meaning. The whole idea is that wisdom is self-contained but, if it loses its ability to stay within itself, it starts to have leakages that are defilements on the wisdom. See also un-outflowed.

Poisons, Tib. dug: poison is a general term for the afflictions. They are, for samsaric beings, poisonous things that afflict the being of the person who has them. The buddha most commonly spoke of the three poisons, which are the principal afflictions of desire, aggression, and ignorance. He also spoke of "the five poisons" which is simply a slightly longer enumeration of the principal afflictions: desire, aggression, delusion, pride, and jealousy.

Post-attainment: see equipoise.

Prajña, Tib. shes rab: a name for a state of mind that makes precise distinctions between this and that. Although it is sometimes translated as "wisdom", that is not correct because it is, generally speaking, a mental event belonging to dualistic mind.

Preserve, Tib. skyong ba: an important term in Thorough Cut. It means to keep something as it is, to nurture something in the sense of keeping it just so and not losing it. In the case of Thorough Cut, it specifically means that you are not using any rational process or effort to keep it in place, rather you are following the instructions received from your guru on allowing it to be as it is. This is also always applied to the state, q.v. and the phrase "preserve the state" is a key oral instruction in the Thorough Cut system.

Rational mind, Tib. blo: the Kagyu and Nyingma traditions use this term pejoratively for the most part. In the Great Completion tradition, blo is the dualistic mind and hence is the villain so to speak which needs to be removed from the equation in order to obtain enlightenment. This term is consistently translated as rational mind throughout this text since merely translating it as mind, which is the common approach these days, utterly loses the importance of the word. This is not just mind but this is the mind that creates the situation of this and that (ratio in Latin) and which is always at the root of all sentient beings problems and which is the very opposite of the essence of mind. This is a key term and it should be noted and not just glossed over as "mind".

Rigpa, Tib. rig pa: The singularly most important term in the whole of Great Completion and Mahāmudrā. This is the term used to indicate enlightened mind as experienced by the practitioner on the path of these practices. The term itself specifically refers to the dynamic knowing quality of mind. It absolutely does not mean a simple registering, as implied by the word "awareness" which unfortunately is often used to translate this term. There is no word in English that exactly matches it, unfortunately, though the idea of "seeing" or "insight on the spot" is very close. Proof of this is found in the fact that the original Sanskrit term "vidyā" is actually the root of all words in English that start with "vid" and mean "to see", for example, "video". Chogyam Trungpa Rinpoche, who was particular skilled at getting Tibetan words into English, also stated that this term rigpa really did not have a good equivalent in English, though "insight" he thought was the closest. My own conclusion after hearing extensive teachings on these subjects is that rigpa is just best left untranslated. However, it will be helpful in reading the text to understanding the meaning as just given. Note that rigpa has both noun and verb forms. To get the verb forms in this book, I have used "rigpa'ing".

Seven Dharmas of Vairochana, Tib. rnam par snang mdzad chos bdun: are the seven aspects of Vairochana's posture which used for formal meditation practice. The posture for the legs is the one called "vajra posture" or vajrāsana. In it, the legs are crossed one on top of the other, right on top of left. The advantage of this posture is that, of the five basic winds of the subtle body, the downward-clearing wind is caused to enter the central channel. The posture for the hands is called the equipoise mudrā. The right palm is placed on top of the left palm and the two thumbs are just touching, raised up over the palms. The advantage of this posture is that the Fire-Accompanying Wind is caused to enter the central channel. The posture for the spine is that the spine should be held straight. The advantage of this posture is that the Pervader Wind is caused to enter the central channel. The posture for the shoulders is one in which the shoulders are held up slightly in a particular way. The advantage of this posture is that Upward-Moving Wind is caused to enter the central channel. The neck and chin are held in a particular posture: the neck is drawn up a little and the chin slightly hooked in towards the throat. The advantage of this posture is that the Life-Holder Wind is caused to enter the central channel. The tip of the tongue is joined with the forward part of the palate and the jaws are relaxed, with the teeth and lips allowed to sit normally. The eyes are directed down past the tip of the nose, into space. Placing the gaze in this way keeps the clarity of mind and prevents sinking, agitation, and so on.

Shamatha, Tib. gzhi gnas: one of the two main practices of meditation required in the Buddhist system for gaining insight into reality. It develops one-pointedness of mind. The completion of the practice is a mind that sits stably on its object without any effort. Essentially, it allows the other practice, vipaśhyanā, to focus on its object unwaveringly.

State, Tib. ngang: this is a key term in Mahāmudrā and Great Completion. Unfortunately it is often not translated and in so doing much meaning is lost. Alternatively, it is often translated as "within" which is incorrect. The term means a "state". A state is an ongoing situation and that is exactly what the Tibetan is referring to. It has the full sense of "a particular state that the practitioner is in". There are many states on the path. In Great Completion, the word is often used in the Thorough Cut without adjective to refer to the all-important experience of the essence of mind, whatever that might be at the time. Hence "the state", "preserving the state", etcetera. See also "Preserve".

Stoppageless, Tib. 'gag pa med pa: A key term of Mahāmudrā and Great Completion that is usually mis-translated. It is usually translated as "unceasing". However, this is a different verb. It refers to the situation in which one thing is not being stopped by another thing. It means "not stopped", "without stoppage", "not blocked and prevented by something else" that is, stoppageless. The verb form associated with it is "not stopped" q.v.

Superfactual Truth, Tib. don dam bden pa: one of a pair of terms; the other is Fictional Truth, q.v. The usual translation as "absolute truth" is not the meaning at all of this key term. The term means the level of reality (*truth*) that is seen by the wisdom of a being who has transcended saṃsāra. This wisdom is *superior* to the ordinary person's consciousness and the *fact*s that appear on its surface are *true* compared to the facts that appear to the mind in the fictional reality of the ordinary person.

Superfice, superficies, Tib. rnam pa: in discussions of mind, a distinction is made between the entity of mind which is a mere knower and the superficial things that appear on its surface and which are known by it. In other words, the superficies are the various things which pass over the surface of mind but which are not mind. Superficies are all the specifics that constitute appearance, for example, the colour white within a moment of visual consciousness, the vroom of a motorbike within an ear consciousness, and so on.

Thorough Cut, Tib. khregs chod: the Dzogchen system has several levels to it. The innermost level has two main practices, the first is Thregcho which literally translates as Thorough Cut and the second is Thogal which translates as Direct Crossing. The meaning of Threkcho has been misunderstood and hence mistranslated. The meaning is clearly explained in the *Illuminator Tibetan-English Dictionary*; it gives the following.

> "The Thorough Cut is a system in which the solidification that sentient beings produce by having rational minds which grasp at a perceived object and perceiving subject is sliced through so as to get the underlying reality which has always been present in the essence of mind and which is called Alpha Purity in this system of teachings. For this reason Thorough Cut is also known as Alpha Purity Thorough Cut."

The etymology of the word is explained in the Great Completion System either as ཁྲེགས་སུ་ཆོད་པ་ or ཁྲེགས་གེ་ཆོད་པ་. In either case, the term ཆོད་པ་ is the standard intransitive verb meaning "for something to be cut through". As the intransitive root, it simply comes to mean "a cut", a type of cut. Some Westerners have tried to make a big deal out of the intransitive sense, suggesting that it means a past tense sense, that is, a cut which has happened. That shows a misunderstanding of Tibetan grammar. The intransitive sense here just makes it "a cut" like in English there could be all sorts of different "cuts". So this is one type of "cut". Then, in the case of ཁྲེགས་སུ་ཆོད་པ་, ཁྲེགས་སུ་ becomes an adverb modifying the verb "to cut" and has the meaning of making the cut fully, completely. It is explained with the example of slicing off a finger. A finger could be sliced with a sharp knife such that the cut was not quite complete and the cut off portion was left hanging. Alternatively, it could be sliced through in one, decisive movement such that the finger was completely and definitely severed. In the case of ཁྲེགས་གེ་ཆོད་པ་, the term ཁྲེགས་གེ་ functions as an adverb though it is one of the many experiential terms of the Tibetan language. It has the meaning and feeling with it, of something that is doubtless, of something that is unquestionably so. A translation based on the first explanation would be "Complete Cut", "Thorough Cut", "Cutting Through", "Through Cut", "Solid Cut". A translation based on the second explanation would be "Definite Cut", "Decisive Cut".

Other translations that have been put forward for this term are: "Cutting Resistance" and "Cutting Solidity". Of these, "Cutting Resistance" is usually a translation made on the basis of students expressing the "resistance to practice", etcetera. That is a complete misunderstanding of the term: firstly the words of the term mean "Decisive Cut" or "Thorough Cut", and secondly, the term refers specifically to decisively cutting the solidification that has happened because of བློ་ rational mind dualizing the world into a perceived object and perceiving subject, with the result of arriving fully and directly into the alpha purity of the ground.

The Thorough Cut" gives the sense that the practitioner of this system cuts decisively through the conceptual solidification which is none other than rational mind so as to arrive directly at the essence of mind.

Three Principal Trainings, Tib. bslabs pa gsum. The three principal trainings of the Buddhist path are śhīla, samādhi, and prajñā —discipline, concentration, and correct discernment.

Three Secrets, Tib. gsang ba: the body, speech, and mind of a person on the way to Buddhahood. When the person becomes a buddha, these have reached their full state of enlightenment and then are usually referred to as the three vajras of a tathāgata. However, sometime the path term is used to refer to the body, speech, and mind of a buddha.

Three Types of Analysis, Tib. dpyad pa gsum: there are three types of inferential reasoning that can be used to assess anything not known with direct perception. One of them is the type of reasoning just mentioned above called Reasoning of the Force of the Thing. The remaining two are reasoning of that relies on the trustworthiness of the thing being examined and the reasoning that relies on popular knowledge concerning the status of the thing being examined. The first type of the three is superior to the others. When a thing is examined with all three types of reasoning and it is discerned to be valid, it is said to be "pure" after application of the three reasonings, a wording that is found in Mipham's commentary.

Transparency, Tib. zang thal: This term belongs to the unique vocabulary of Great Completion. It has two parts to its meaning: the first is that something is seen directly, in direct perception; the second part is that it is seen with full visibility because there is no obscuring agent in the way at all. The term is used to indicate that rigpa is truly present for the practitioner. Luminosity when it is the rigpa of the enlightened side and not the not-rigpa, usually translated as ignorance, of the samsaric side, has transparency or, you could say, full visibility, as one of its qualities precisely because it has none of the factors of mind as such in it, which would obscure it. In this condition. For the practitioner, transparency means that the rigpa is in full view because it really is rigpa without any of the obscuring factors that would make it opaque and not completely visible.

Unaltered or uncontrived, Tib. ma bcos pa: the opposite of "altered" and "contrived". Something which has not been altered from its native state; something which has been left just as it is.

Upadesha, Tib. man ngag: see glossary entry "Foremost Instructions".

Un-outflowed, Skt. asrava, Tib. zag pa med pa: see also "outflowed". Un-outflowed dharmas are ones that are connected with wisdom that has not lost its footing and leaked out into a defiled state; it is self-contained wisdom that is seeing reality as it is.

Vacillatory focus, Tib. gza' gtad: this is a term which is twice pejorative. The word "vacillatory" refers to a process of hovering around a subject, seeing it from this angle and that angle because of being uncertain of which way it really is; that is, vacillating over which way it is. "Focus" means that rational-mind takes one of the possible angles and settles on that. For example, in the process of resting in the essence of mind, there can be the fault of not leaving rational mind but staying within in it and thinking, "Yes, this is the essence of mind" or "No, this is not it. It is that". Each of those is a vacillatory focus. Any vacillatory focus implies that the practitioner has not left rational mind and so is not in rigpa.

Vajra Vehicle, Skt. vajrayāna, Tib. rdo rje'i theg pa: see under Great Vehicle.

Vehicle of Characteristics, Tib. mtshan nyid theg pa: another name for the conventional Great Vehicle. See under Great Vehicle. It is called the Vehicle of Characteristics because the teachings in it rely on a conventional approach in which logic is used to find reality and in doing so, the characteristics of phenomena are a key part of the explanations of the system.

View, meditation, and conduct, Tib. lta sgom spyod: a formulation of the teachings that contains all of the meaning of the path.

Vipashyana, Tib. lhag mthong: one of the two main practices of meditation required in the Buddhist system for gaining insight into reality. It is the insight that directly sees reality. It is aided by śhamatha which keeps it focussed on the reality.

Wisdom, Tib. ye shes: this terms translates the original Sanskrit, jñāna. Jñāna has many meanings but overall has the sense of just knowing. In the Buddhist usage it is very literal, meaning the most basic sense we have of knowing which is the knowing that is there from the beginning in the core of mind.

Because of this meaning, the Tibetans translated it as "the particular awareness which has been there from the beginning". This has been translated into English in various ways but, as long as the meaning just mentioned is understood, that will be enough.

In the tantras, there are many methods for bringing the students to this primordial awareness. Some of them bring the student first to something which is similar to the wisdom so there is the term, simile wisdom[73]; this is often translated as example wisdom but that is being literal to the extent of losing the meaning. The simile wisdom is a similitude of the real wisdom, the actual wisdom which is shown in various ways, including by the fourth empowerment. Real wisdom[74] is the opposite of simile wisdom; it is wisdom in fact, not the one which is just a similitude of the real wisdom.

---

[73] Tib. dpe'i ye shes

[74] Tib. don gyi ye shes

TIBETAN TEXTS

༄༅། །ཐུན་མོང་མ་ཡིན་པའི་སེམས་ཁྲིད་ཉུང་བསྡུས་ཐར་པའི་སྒོ་འབྱེད་བཞུགས་སོ།།

༄༅། །ན་མོ་གུ་རུ། ཐོག་མའི་མགོན་པོ་དང་དབྱེར་མ་མཆིས་པ་ཁྱབ་བདག་བསྟན་པའི་ཉི་མ་རིན་པོ་ཆེའི་ཞབས་ལ་སྒོ་གསུམ་གུས་པ་ཆེན་པོས་ཕྱག་འཚལ་ལོ། །འདིར་སེམས་ཀྱི་གནས་ལུགས་སྐྱོང་ཚུལ་ཙུང་ཟད་བྲི་བ་ལ་བཀའི་གནང་བ་སྩོལ་ལ་བྱིན་གྱིས་རློབས། དེ་ལ་སྔོན་འགྲོ། དངོས་གཞི་གཉིས་ལས། དང་པོ་ཐུན་མོང་གི་སྔོན་འགྲོ་དལ་འབྱོར་རྙེད་དཀའ་བ། འཆི་བ་མི་རྟག་པ། ལས་རྒྱུ་འབྲས། འཁོར་བའི་ཉེས་དམིགས་རྣམས་ལ་ཡིད་ཆེས་ཀྱི་བློ་སྦྱངས་ནས་འཁོར་བ་ལ་ཞེན་པ་མ་ལོག་བར་དུ་བསྒོམ། ཐུན་མོང་མ་ཡིན་པའི་སྔོན་འགྲོའི་ཆོས་སྐྱབས་འགྲོ་ཕྱག་སྦྲགས། རྡོར་སེམས་སྒོམ་བཟླས། མཎྜལ། བླ་མའི་རྣལ་འབྱོར་རྣམས་རྫོགས་ཆེན་སྤྱི་ལྟར་རྟགས་ཐོན་བྱ། གཉིས་པ་དངོས་གཞི་ཡའང་ལུས་ཀྱི་འདུག་སྟངས། བླ་མའི་བྱིན་འབེབས། སེམས་ཀྱི་ལྟ་ཐབས་གསུམ་ལས། དང་པོ་ལུས་རྣམ་སྣང་གི་ཆོས་བདུན་བྱ། གཉིས་པ་བླ་མའི་བྱིན་འབེབས་ནི། རང་ཉིད་སྐད

ཅིག་གིས་ཆེ་མཆོག་ཡབ་ཡུམ་གསལ་བའི་སྤྱི་བོར་པདྨ་དང་ཟླ་བའི་གདན་ལ་ངོ་བོ་རྩ་བའི་བླ་མ་ལ། རྣམ་པ་དཔལ་ཀུན་ཏུ་བཟང་པོ་སྐུ་མདོག་མཐིང་ག་ཆོས་སྐུའི་ཆ་ལུགས་ཅན་ཕྱག་མཉམ་བཞག་མཚན་དང་དཔེ་བྱད་ཀྱིས་བརྒྱན་ནས་ཡུམ་ཆོས་དབྱིངས་ཀུན་ཏུ་བཟང་མོ་དཀར་མོ་དང་སྦྱོར་བ། འཇའ་འོད་རྣམ་ལྔ་འཁྲུགས་པའི་ཀློང་དུ་བཞུགས་པ་གསལ་གདབ་ལ་སྙིང་ཁྲུང་རུས་པའི་གཏིང་ནས་གསོལ་བ་འདེབས་ཤིང་ངག་གིས་ཀྱང་འདི་ཉིད་བརྗོད་པར་བྱ། འདི་ཕྱིའི་སྐྱབས་མགོན་དྲིན་ཅན་བླ་མ་རྗེར། །སྒོ་གསུམ་གུས་པ་ཆེན་པོའི་གསོལ་བ་འདེབས། །ཀ་དག་རིག་སྟོང་རང་ངོ་འཕྲོད་པ་དང་། །ཐོད་རྒལ་སྣང་བ་བཞི་པོ་རྩལ་རྫོགས་ནས། །འཇའ་ལུས་འོད་ཕུང་འགྲུབ་པར་བྱིན་གྱིས་རློབས། །ཞེས་ལུས་བ་སྤུ་ལྡང་། གདོང་མཆི་མ་མ་འཁྲུགས་ཀྱི་བར་དུ་གསོལ་བ་ནན་གྱིས་བཏབ་མཐར། དཔལ་ལྡན་བླ་མའི་དཔྲལ་བའི་ཨོཾ་དཀར་ལས། །འོད་ཟེར་དཀར་པོ་ལུ་གུ་རྒྱུད་དུ་འཕྲོས། །བདག་གི་དཔྲལ་བའི་ཐིག་ལེ་དཀར་པོར་ཞུགས། །ཐིག་ལེ་དེ་ཉིད་ཨོཾ་ཡིག་ཞལ་གྱིས་སོང་། །ཚེ་རབས་ལུས་ཀྱི་སྡིག་སྒྲིབ་མ་ལུས་དག །འགྲོ་འདུལ་སྤྲུལ་སྐུ་ཐོབ་པར་བྱིན་གྱིས་རློབས། །དཔལ་ལྡན་བླ་མའི་མགྲིན་པར་ཨཱཿདམར་ལས། །འོད་ཟེར་དམར་པོ་ལུ་གུ་རྒྱུད་དུ་འཕྲོས། །བདག་གིས་མགྲིན་པའི་ཐིག་ལེ་དམར་པོར་ཞུགས། །ཐིག་ལེ་དེ་ཉིད་ཨཱཿཡིག་ཞལ་གྱིས་སོང་། །ཚེ་རབས་ངག་གི་སྡིག་སྒྲིབ་མ་ལུས་དག །འགག་མེད་ལོངས་སྐུ་ཐོབ་པར་བྱིན་གྱིས་རློབས། །དཔལ་ལྡན་བླ་མའི་ཐུགས་ཀའི་ཧཱུྃ་མཐིང་ལས། །འོད་ཟེར་སྔོན་པོ་ལུ་གུ་རྒྱུད་དུ་འཕྲོས། །བདག་གི་སྙིང་གི་ཐིག་ལེ་སྔོན་པོར་ཞུགས། །ཐིག་ལེ་དེ་ཉིད་ཧཱུྃ་ཡིག་ཞལ་གྱིས་སོང་། །ཚེ་རབས་ཡིད་ཀྱི་སྡིག་སྒྲིབ་མ་ལུས་དག །སྐྱེ་མེད་ཆོས་སྐུ་ཐོབ་པར་བྱིན་གྱིས་རློབས། །དཔལ་ལྡན་བླ

མའི་ལྟེ་བའི་ཧྲཱིཿདམར་ལས། །འོད་ཟེར་རྣམ་ལྔ་ལུ་གུ་རྒྱུད་དུ་འཕྲོས། །
བདག་གི་ལྟེ་བའི་ཐིག་ལེ་དམར་པོར་ཞུགས། །ཐིག་ལེ་དེ་ཉིད་ཧྲཱིཿཡིག་ཞལ་
གྱིས་སོང་། །བློ་གསུམ་ཆ་མཉམ་སྡིག་སྒྲིབ་མ་ལུས་དག །ངོ་བོ་ཉིད་སྐུ་
ཐོབ་པར་བྱིན་གྱིས་རློབས། །མཐར་ནི་མོས་གུས་གདུང་ཤུགས་དྲག་པོ་
ཡིས། །བླ་མ་ཡབ་ཡུམ་འོད་ཀྱི་གོང་བུར་ཞུ། །རིག་པའི་ཀློང་དུ་དབྱེར་
མེད་གཅིག་ཏུ་འདྲེས། །སྨྲ་བསམ་བརྗོད་མེད་ཀུན་བཟང་ཐུགས་ཀློང་ཨ།
ཞེས་པས་ཐུགས་ཡིད་ཅིག་ཆར་བསྲེ་བའི་མཐར་ཅི་གནས་སུ་བཞག །འཇུ་བའི་ཚེ་ངོ་བོ་ལ་
ཅེར་གྱི་བལྟའོ། །གསུམ་པ་དངོས་གཞི་ལའང་མཚན་མ་ལ་བརྟེན་ནས་ཞི་
གནས་བཙལ་བ་དང་། མཚན་མེད་ལ་བརྟེན་ནས་ཞི་གནས་སྐྱོང་བ་གཉིས་
ལས། དང་པོ་རང་གི་མདུན་དུ་རྡེའུ་གཅིག་བཞག་ནས་དེ་ལ་མིག་དང་ཤེས་པ་
མ་ཡེངས་པར་རྩེ་གཅིག་ཏུ་བལྟ། མི་གནས་པར་འཕྲོ་ན་རྣམ་རྟོག་དང་མིག་
རྩེལ་བསྲེ་ནས་བལྟ། ཡུན་ཐུང་ཙམ་ནས་ངལ་བསོ། དེ་བཞིན་གྱི་སྔར་
བས་གནས་ཉམས་ཆེ་ཙམ་མ་བྱུང་བར་ཡུན་ཐུང་གྲངས་མང་གིས་བལྟ། དེ་
མཚམས་རང་གི་སྙིང་ཁར་ཧཱུྃ་ཡིག་མཐིང་ག་ཞིག་གསལ། དེ་ལས་ཧཱུྃ་མང་
པོ་བར་མ་ཆད་པར་འཕྲོས་པའི་སྔར་གྱི་རྡེའུ་ལ་གཡས་སྐོར་གྱིས་ཚུལ་དུ་ཧཱུྃ་ཐོག་
རྡེའུའི་སྟེང་དུ་སོང་བ་ལ་རིག་པ་གཏད། དེ་ནས་ཧཱུྃ་རྣམས་རིམ་པར་ཚུར་ལྡོག་
ནས་སྙིང་ཁའི་ཧཱུྃ་ལ་ཐིམ་པར་བསྒོམ། ཡང་ངལ་བསོ། དེ་ལ་ཡིད་
གོམས་པ་ཙམ་བསྒོམ། དེ་ནས་རང་ལུས་དེ་ཧཱུྃ་ཡིག་སྔོན་པོ་ཞིག་ཏུ་གྱུར་ནས་
ས་ལ་མ་རེག་ཙམ་ནས་རིམ་པས་ལམ་དང་རིའི་ཕ་ཚད་དུ་བཏང་། མ་བརྗེད་
ཙམ་གྱི་ཐོག་ནས་ངལ་བསོ། ཡང་སྔར་བཞིན་ཚུར་ལྡོག དེ་འདྲ་ལན་མང་
དུ་བསྒོམ། དེ་མཚམས་རང་གི་སྙིང་ག་དང་། མདུན་དུ་ཧཱུྃ་རེ་བསྒོམ།
སྙིང་གའི་ཧཱུྃ་ལས་ཧཱུྃ་གཅིག་འཕྲོས། མདུན་གྱི་ཧཱུྃ་ལ་ཐོག ཧཱུྃ་དེ་བཀྲག་

མདངས་ཆེར་འབར་ཚོངས་སྨྲུག་ནས་ཞུགས་ཧེ་སླིང་གའི་ཧཱུྃ་ལ་ཐིམ་པར་བསྒོམ། དེ་ལ་བརྟན་པ་ཐོབ་པ་ཙམ་བསྒོམ། དེ་གནས་པ་ལ་ཙུང་ཟད་ཕན་འོང་། འདི་ནི་མཚན་ཅན་གྱི་ཞི་གནས་སོ། །གཉིས་པ་མཚན་མེད་ཀྱི་ཞི་གནས་སྐྱོང་བ་ལ། ལུས་གནད་ལྟ་སྟངས་སྔར་ལྟར། བཀའ་དྲིན་འཁོར་མེད་བླ་མ་སྤྱི་བོར་བསྒོམ། གསོལ་བ་རྩེ་གཅིག་ཏུ་གདབ། རང་ལ་བསྟིམ་པའི་མཐར་རིག་པ་གློད་ཀྱིས་འཇོག་པའི་དུས་ཙུང་ཟད་སྟོང་ཧྲུམ་མེར་འགྲོ་བ་དེ་གནས་པ། དེའི་ངང་ནས་རྣམ་རྟོག་ཁྱུར་ཁྱུར་གྱིས་འཕྲོ་བ་དེ་འགྱུ་བ། གནས་འགྱུའི་རྩད་ཆོད་མཁན་དེ་རིག་པ། དེ་ལ་རྒྱུན་བསྲིངས་པས་དང་པོ་རྣམ་རྟོག་ཇེ་མང་དུ་འགྲོ་བའི་ཚེ་གནས་པ་དང་པོ་ཡིན་པས་དེ་ལ་ངང་མ་ཆད་པར་སྐྱོང་བས་རྣམ་རྟོག་ཇེ་དལ་དང་གནས་པ་ཇེ་ཆེར་འགྲོ། འགྱུས་ཀྱང་གནས་པ་ལ་ཆེར་མི་གནོད་པ་འོང་། དེ་ལ་གནས་པ་བར་མ་ཟེར། དེ་ལྟར་རྒྱུན་བར་བསྐྱངས་པས། མཐར་ཡུན་ཇི་ཙམ་བཞག་འདོད་པ་དེ་ཙམ་དུ་གནས་པ་ཞིག་འོང་། དེའི་དུས་སྣང་བ་བདེ་སང་ངེ་། གསལ་ཤལ་ལེ། རྣམ་རྟོག་ཙུང་ཟད་འཕྲོས་ཀྱང་མི་གནོད་པར་གནས་པ་དེ་ལ་ཞི་གནས་ཟེར། དེ་ཉིད་བརྟན་པ་ཐོབ་པ་ཞིག་ཤིན་ཏུ་གནད་གལ་ཆེ། དེའི་ངོ་བོ་ལ་བལྟས་ཙ་ན་རྣམ་རྟོག་ལྷག་གེར་ཤར་བ་དེ་ལ་ཅེར་གྱིས་བལྟས་པས་སྟོང་ཧྲུམ་གྱི་འགྲོ་བ་དེ་ཉིད་ལྷག་མཐོང་ཤར་བ་ཡིན། དེ་ལ་རྒྱུན་པར་སྐྱོང་བས་བདེ་གསལ་གྱི་ཉམས་ཇེ་ཆེར་འགྲོ། དེ་ལ་མ་ཆགས་པར་ངོ་བོ་ལ་ལྟ་བ་གལ་ཆེ། དེ་ལྟར་སྐྱོང་བའི་གནས་འགྱུ་རིག་གསུམ་གཅིག་ཏུ་འདྲེས་ནས་རྣམ་རྟོག་འགྱུས་ཀྱང་སྟོང་པར་ཡོང་། འདི་རྩེ་གཅིག་ཆེན་པོ་ཡིན་སྙམ། འདི་སྐབས་གཉིད་དུ་ཡོལ་ཚེ་གཡང་དུ་ལྷུང་བའམ། རྨི་ལམ་སྐྲག་པ་ཞིག་རྨིས་ནས་དེའི་རྐྱེན་བྱེད་དེ་རྨི་ལམ་དེ་ཁའི་ཐོག་ཏུ་གསལ་ཧྲུམ་མེར་ཡུན་རིང་དུ་གནས་པའི་མཐར་སད་རྒྱུ་རེ་ཡོད་པ་འགའ་ཙམ་འོང་བས་འོད་

གསལ་ཨེ་ཡིན་སླམ། དེ་སྐབས་རྒྱུན་པར་དྲན་རྫི་མ་གཏོགས་ཅི་ཡང་བསྒོམ་
དུ་མེད་པ་ཞིག་འབྱུང་། ཐང་འགར་གཉིད་པའི་ཚེ་འོད་ཟླ་ཐིག་ལྟ་བུ་ཞིག་ཤར་
བ་དེ་ཧེ་ཆེར་སོང་ནས་ཁྱིམ་ཀུན་གསལ་བ་ཉིན་མོའི་སྣང་བ་ལྟར་འབྱུང་།
གོང་གི་འོད་གསལ་དང་འདི་གཉིས་སྤེལ་མ་འདྲ་བར་འོང་བར་མངོན་ནོ། །དེ་
ནས་བླ་མ་ལ་མོས་གུས་ཞུར་ཚུགས་སུ་བྱས་ནས་བསྐྱང་བས། སྔར་ཡོད་པའི་
བདེ་གསལ་གྱི་ཉམས་དེ་གཏན་ནས་མེད་པ། གནས་པའང་ཧ་ཅང་མི་ཆེ་བ།
འདི་ཡིན་དེ་མིན་མེད་པ། གནས་མ་གནས། སྟོང་མ་སྟོང་གི་འཛིན་པ་
མེད་པ། རང་ཡང་ཐེ་ཚོམ་སྐྱེས་པ་གཉིད་པའི་ཚེ་ཕྱི་ཡུལ་དང་རང་ལུས་སྟོང་
པར་འགྲོ་བ་དེའི་སྐབས་སྐྲག་སྔངས་ཀྱིས་གཉིད་ཧར་སད་དུ་ཡོང་བ། ཉིན་
མོའི་དུས་མ་ཡེངས་ཙམ་མ་གཏོགས་བྱ་རྒྱུ་ཅི་ཡང་མེད་པ་ཞིག་འོང་། དེ་མུས་
སུ་རྟག་པར་སྐྱོང་བ་གནད་དོ། །སྐབས་སྐབས་སུ་རྣམ་རྟོག་ཁྱུར་ཁྱུར་གྱིས་
བྱུང་ན་ཕཊ༔ དྲག་པོ་བརྗོད་ཅིང་ངོ་བོ་ལ་ཅེར་གྱིས་བལྟ། སྐབས་སྐབས་
ཕཊ༔ དྲག་པོ་རེ་བརྗོད་ཅིང་དབྱིངས་རིག་བསྲེ་ལ་ལྟ་སྟངས་དབྱིངས་སུ་གཏད།
དེ་ལྟར་བསྒོམ་པས་རིག་པ་དང་ཕྱི་སྣང་གཉིས་སོ་སོར་ཕྱེ་རྒྱུ་མེད་པ་ཞིག་འབྱུང་།
མ་ཡེངས་སྐབས་སུ་ཚོགས་བརྒྱད་ཀྱི་ཡུལ་སྣང་ཐམས་ཅད་འདི་ཡིན་དེ་མིན་གྱི་
དངོས་པོར་གཟུང་རྒྱུ་མེད་པ་སྟོང་ཁྲམ་མེར་འགྲོ་བ་ཞིག་འོང་། ཡེངས་
སྐབས་དེ་ལྟར་མི་འབྱུང་། འདི་དུས་ཡེངས་སྐབས་བརྗེད་སྐབས་ཤིན་ཏུ་མང་
བས་དྲན་རྫིས་ངོ་བོ་སྐྱོང་བ་ཡང་ཡང་བྱ་རྒྱུ་གནད་གལ་ཆེ། འདི་སྐབས་གཉིད་
དུས་ཀྱང་རེས་འགའ་གསལ་བ་ཙམ་གྱིས་འོད་གསལ་ཟིན་པ་དང་། རེས་
འགའ་གསལ་བ་མེད་པར་སྟོང་ཁྲམ་མེར་འགྲོ་བ་དང་། རེས་འགའ་གསལ་
བ་དེས་རང་དང་ཉེ་སྐོར་ཙམ་སྣང་བ། རེས་འགའ་རྨི་ལམ་རིག་པའི་ཀློང་དུ་
རང་ཤར་རང་གྲོལ་དུ་འགྲོ་བ་ཞིག་འབྱུང་། འཆར་ཚུལ་དེ་རྣམས་ཐ་མལ་གྱི་

ཞེས་པའི། སངས་རྒྱས་ཀྱི་དགོངས་པ་སེམས་ཅན་གྱི་གནས་ལུགས། ཆོས་སྐུའི་ངོ་བོ་གཅེར་མཐོང་དུ་ངོ་འཕྲོད་པ་ཡིན་ནམ་སླམ་པ། ཁྲེགས་ཆོད་ཀྱི་གནས་ལུགས་རྟོགས། ཐོད་རྒལ་གྱི་རྩལ་འབྱོངས་ནས་གདོས་བཅས་འོད་ཕུང་དུ་གྲོལ་ཚུལ་རྫོགས་པ་ཆེན་པོའི་གཞུང་ན་གསལ། འདིའི་ཐོག་མཐའ་བར་གསུམ་གྱི་ཉམས་མྱོང་སྐྱེ་མི་སྐྱེ་གནས་ལུགས་རྟོགས་མི་རྟོགས། གེགས་དང་གོལ་ས་ཡོད་མེད་སོགས་བླ་མའི་མོས་གུས་ཁོ་ན་ལ་རག་ལས་པས་སྤྲང་རྒན་བདག་གིས་ཀྱང་བླ་མ་ཁོ་ན་ལ་གསོལ་བ་བཏབ། མོས་གུས་ཕུར་ཚུགས་སུ་བྱུས་པས་བླ་མའི་བྱིན་གྱི་རྟོགས་པ་ཅུང་ཟད་ཙམ་རྒྱུད་ལ་སྐྱེ་བ་བྱུང་། ཕྱི་རབས་ཉམས་ལེན་བྱེད་མི་རྣམས་ཀྱང་བླ་མའི་མོས་གུས་ལ་འབད་ན་གདམས་པ་ཀུན་གྱི་ཟབ་གནད་འདི་ལ་ཡོད་པར་འདུག་པས་ཀུན་གྱིས་བླ་མ་ལ་གསོལ་བ་འདེབས་པ་གཅེས་སོ། །སེམས་ངོ་རྟོགས་ཀྱང་བོགས་མ་ཐོན་ན་རྟོགས་པ་ན་མི་འཕར་བས། བོགས་འདོན་འདི་གལ་ཤིན་ཏུ་ཆེ་བས་བོགས་འདོན་གྱི་མཆོག་ནི་བླ་མའི་མོས་གུས་ཡིན་པས་བླ་མ་སྤྱི་བོར་བསྒོམ། གསོལ་བ་ཕུར་ཚུགས་སུ་བཏབ། ཐུགས་ཡིད་མ་འདྲེས་བར་ནན་གྱིས་བསྒོམ། དེས་བོགས་ངེས་པར་ཐོན། དེ་ནས་དུག་ལྔ་དྲག་པ་རེ་སྐྱེས་པའི་ཚེ་མི་དགག་ན་དེའི་ངོ་བོ་ལ་ཅེར་གྱིས་བལྟས་པའི་ཚེ་སྟོང་ཁྲུམ་མེར་འགྲོ། དེ་ཡེ་ཤེས་ཡིན། གཞན་མ་ཉེས་ཁ་ཡོགས་སོགས་མི་བཟོད་པའི་ཚིག་ངན་ཐོས་ཚེ་དེའི་ངོ་བོ་ལ་བལྟས་པས་གྲོལ་ནུས་ན། དེས་བོགས་ཆེན་པོ་འབྱུང་ངོ་། །ལས་དང་པོ་པའི་སེམས་ངོ་སྐྱོང་བའི་ཚེ། བྱིང་རྨུག་འཐིབ་པ་སོགས་མང་བས་དེའི་སྐྱོན་སེལ་ཐབས་ནི་རིག་པ་རྒོད་ན་ལུས་སེམས་གློད་ཀྱི་འཛོག ལྟ་སྟངས་ཟིམ་བུས་གདན་མཚམས་སུ་གཏད། འཐིབ་ན་ལྟ་སྟངས་དབྱིངས་སུ་གཏད། རིག་པ་ཙུང་ཟད་བསྒྲིམ། བྱིང་ན་མིག་འབྲས་ཕྱེན་དུ་ལྡོག རྣམ་རྟོག་

གཅིག་སྐྱེས་གཉིས་སྐྱེས་རིག་པ་གློད་ཀྱིས་ངོས་འཛིན་པ་གལ་ཆེ། དེ་ལྟར་བྱས་པས་སྐྱོན་རྣམས་སེལ་ལོ། །དེ་ལྟར་སེམས་ལ་ཕན་པའི་གདམས་ངག་ཟབ་མོ་ཞིག་དགོས་ཞེས་མཆེད་གྲོགས་ཆོས་འཕེལ་གྱིས་ནན་དུ་བསྐུལ་བས་རང་ལ་ཡོན་ཏན་ཆ་ཙམ་རྒྱུད་ལ་མེད་ཅིང་། ༄ དྲེད་པོ་ངོས་ལྐོག་མཁན་བདག་འདྲ་བས་ཐོབ་རྫུན་སྨྲ་བར་མི་འོས་ཀྱང་། བསྐུལ་བ་པོའི་ངོ་ལྡོག་མ་ནུས་པས་སྐྱབས་གནས་བཀའ་དྲིན་འཁོར་མེད་བསྟན་པའི་ཉི་མ་ལ་གསོལ་བ་བཏབ་ནས་སྤྲང་རྒན་ཤཱཀྱ་ཤྲཱིས་དགོན་ཐུན་སྒྲོན་མེའི་ངོགས་སུ་བྲིས། སེམས་ལ་ཕན་པའི་ཁྲིད་ཡིག་ཉུང་བསྡུས་འདི། །རང་འདྲ་བློ་དམན་འགའ་ལ་ཕན་དྲན། །ཉེས་འགལ་མཆིས་ན་ཀུན་བཟང་ཀློང་དུ་བཤགས། །དགེ་བས་འགྲོ་ཀུན་སྨིན་ཅིང་གྲོལ་གྱུར་ཅིག །ཨེ་ཀ་པྲ་ཏི་ཛྙོར།། །།

ཨོཾ༔ ཐེག་པའི་རྩེ་རྒྱལ་ཨ་ཏི་རྫོགས་པ་ཆེན་པོ་ལས༔ ཁྲེགས་ཆོད་ཀྱི་གསང་ལམ་སྙིང་གི་དུམ་བུ་གཉིས་པ་རིག་པ་གཅེར་མཐོང་གི་གདམས་པ་བཞུགས་སོ།།

༄༔ གདོད་མའི་མགོན་པོ་གུ་རུ་བདེ་བ་ཆེན་པོའི་སྐུ་ལ་ཕྱག་འཚལ་ཞིང་སྐྱབས་སུ་མཆིའོ༔ འདིར་ཡང་གསང་བླ་མ་བདེ་བ་ཆེན་པོའི་སྒྲུབ་པའི་སྐོར་ལ༔ གསང་བ་ལམ་གྱི་རིམ་པ་ལ༔ ཀ་དག་ཁྲེགས་ཆོད་དང་ལྷུན་གྲུབ་ཐོད་རྒལ་གྱི་ཁྲིད་གཉིས་ལས༔ འདིར་ཁྲེགས་ཆོད་ཀྱི་གདམས་པ་ལ༔ སྔོན་འགྲོ་བྱུང་གནས་འགྲོ་གསུམ་རྩད་གཅོད་པ་དང་༔ དངོས་གཞི་ཀ་དག་གི་རིག་པ་ལ་འབེབས་པ༔ རྗེས་རིག་པ་ཀ་དག་གི་རྩལ་ཇི་ལྟར་རྫོགས་པའི་ཚུལ་དང་གསུམ་ལས༔ ཐོག་མར་ཐུན་འགོར་བླ་མའི་རྣལ་འབྱོར་ནི༔ རང་གི་སྒོ་གསུམ་སྤྲོས་པ་དང་བྲལ་བའི་དབྱིངས་ལས༔ རང་སྣང་འགག་པ་མེད་པའི་རྩལ་རང་རིག་ཡེ་ཤེས་ཀྱི་མཁའ་འགྲོ་མ་སྐུ་མདོག་དཀར་ལ་དམར་བའི་མདངས་

དང་ལྡན་པ༔ འཇོམ་ཞིང་ཆགས་པའི་ཉམས་ཅན་དབུ་སྐྲ་སིལ་བུར་འཁྲོལ་
ཞིང་། །ཕྱག་གཡས་གསང་བའི་ཅང་ཏེའུ་ནམ་མཁའ་ལ་སྒྲོག་པ༔
གཡོན་ཟག་མེད་བདུད་རྩིའི་བཅུད་ཀྱིས་གཏམས་པའི་དུང་ཞལ་ཐུགས་ཀར་
བསྣམས་པ༔ རུས་པའི་ཕྱག་རྒྱ་ལྡུས་སྦྲུས་ཤིང་ཟླ་ག་དང་ཉུ་མ་ཤིན་ཏུ་རྒྱུས
པ། པདྨ་དང་ཟླ་བའི་གདན་ལ་གར་སྟབས་ཀྱིས་བཞུགས་པ༔ དེའི་སྟེང་
གི་ཆར་མདུན་གྱི་ནམ་མཁའ་ལ་པདྨ་འབུམ་བརྡལ་ཟླ་བའི་དཀྱིལ་འཁོར་གྱི་
གདན་ལ་སྐྱབས་གནས་ཀུན་འདུས་ཀྱི་བདག་ཉིད་རྡོ་རྗེ་དྲིན་ཆེན་རྩ་བའི་བླ་མ་རྣམ་
པ་གུ་རུ་བདེ་བ་ཆེན་པོ་སྐུ་མདོག་དཀར་པོ་མཚན་དཔེ་དུ་མས་བརྒྱན་ལ་ཤིན་ཏུ་ཞི་
ཞིང་འཛུམ་པ༔ སྤྱན་ཟླུམ་འཁྱིལ་ནམ་མཁའི་དབྱིངས་སུ་གཟིགས་པ༔
དབུ་ལ་པད་ཞྭ་གསོལ་ཞིང་༔ སྐུ་ལ་གསང་གོས་དཀར་པོ་ཕོད་ཀ་མཐིང་ནག
ཆོས་གོས་གསེར་གྱི་པ་ཏྲ་རིས་རྣམས་བརྩེགས་མར་གསོལ་བ༔ ཕྱག་གཉིས
མཉམ་བཞག་གི་སྟེང་ན་འཆི་མེད་བདུད་རྩིའི་བཅུད་ཀྱིས་གཏམས་པའི་ཐོད་ཞལ
བསྣམས་པ༔ ཞབས་མཉམ་པའི་སྐྱིལ་ཀྲུང་གིས་འཇའ་འོད་ཐིག་ལེ་ཟེར་ཐག
ལུ་གུ་རྒྱུད་འབྲུགས་པའི་ཀློང་ན་དགྱེས་ཡེ་རེ་བཞུགས་པ་རྩེ་གཅིག་ཏུ་གསལ
བཏབ་ནས༔ ལུས་གུས་པའི་བ་སྤུ་ལྡང་ཞིང་མཆི་མ་འཁྲུགས་པ༔ ངག
གདུང་ཤུགས་དྲག་པོའི་འོ་དོད་དང་༔ སྙན་པའི་དབྱངས་ཀྱི་རྟ་ལ་དྲངས་ནས
གསོལ་བ་འདེབས༔ སེམས་མོས་གུས་བཟོད་མེད་དྲག་པོས་བླ་མ་ལ་སངས
རྒྱས་དངོས་ཀྱི་འདུ་ཤེས་དང་མ་བྲལ་བའི་ངང་ནས་གསོལ་འདེབས་ཅི་རིགས་པ
བརྗོད་པའི་མཐར་བླ་མ་འོད་ཀྱི་གོང་བུར་ཞུར་ནས་རང་ལ་ཐིམ༔ རང་གི་སྒོ
གསུམ་དང་བླ་མའི་སྐུ་གསུང་ཐུགས་དབྱེར་མེད་པའི་ངང་ལ་ངལ་བསོ་ལ་ཅུང
ཟད་མཉམ་པར་བཞག༔ དེའི་ངང་ནས་རྣམ་རྟོག་ཐོལ་གྱིས་བྱུང་ན༔ དང
པོ་བྱུང་ས་དངོས་པོའི་ཆ་རང་གི་ཕུང་ཁམས་སྐྱེ་མཆེད༔ བརྟན་པ་སྣོད་ཀྱི

འཇིག་རྟེན༔ གཡོ་བ་བཅུད་ཀྱི་སེམས་ཅན་སོགས་གང་ལས་བྱུང་ལེགས་པར་བརྟག་དཔྱད་བྱས་ནས༔ དངོས་པོའི་ཆ་ནས་བྱུང་ས་མ་རྙེད་ན༔ དངོས་མེད་ནམ་མཁའ་སྟོང་པ་སྟེ་སྟེང་འོག་ཕྱོགས་མཚམས་སོགས་གང་ནས་བྱུང་ལེགས་པར་བརྟགས༔ བར་དུ་གནས་ས་རང་གི་ཕུང་ཁམས་སྐྱེ་མཆེད་ཕྱི་ཤ་གཟུགས་དྲུག་ནང་ཤ་བུ་དགུ་མགོ་རལ་རྩེ་རྐང་གི་རྩེ་སོགས་གང་དུ་གནས༔ གནས་ན་གནས་ཚུལ་ཇི་ལྟ་བ་ཞིག་འདུག་ལེགས་པར་དཔྱད༔ ཐ་མ་འགྲོ་བའི་ཡུལ་ཕྱི་ཚོགས་དྲུག་གི་ཡུལ་དབང་པོའི་སྒོ་ལྔ་སོགས་གང་དུ་འགྲོ༔ འགྲོ་བའི་ཚུལ་ཇི་ལྟ་བུ་ཞིག་འདུག་བརྟག་དཔྱད་ལེགས་པར་ཕུ་ཐག་མ་ཆོད་བར་དུ་ནན་ཞར་བྱེད༔ བར་དུ་རང་གི་སེམས་སངས་རྒྱས་མཁན་ངན་སོང་ལ་ལྟུང་མཁན་བདེ་སྡུག་ཚོར་མཁན་འདི་ཉིད་དངོས་པོ་ཞིག་འདུག་གམ་དངོས་མེད་འདུག༔ དངོས་པོ་ཞིག་འདུག་ན་གཟུགས་ཁ་དོག་དབྱིབས་མཚན་ཉིད་ཇི་ལྟ་བུ་འདུག་ལེགས་པར་བརྟགས་ཞིང་དཔྱད༔ དངོས་མེད་རེད་སྙམ་ན་ནམ་མཁའ་སྟོང་པ་ལ་འདུ་ཤེས་མེད་པར་གཞིར་བཅས་པས༔ སེམས་བདེ་སྡུག་འཁྲུག་ལྡོག་སྒོམ་གསུམ་སོགས་མྱོང་མཁན་འདི་ཇི་ལྟ་བུ་ཞིག་འདུག་ལེགས་པར་བརྟགས་ཞིང་དཔྱད༔ ཐ་མ་དཔྱད་པའི་ཡུལ་དང་དཔྱོད་མཁན་གྱི་འདུ་ཤེས་གཉིས་པོ་གཅིག་གམ་ཐ་དད༔ གཅིག་གོ་སྙམ་ན་གཅིག་པོ་དེ་ལ་མཚན་ཉིད་ཇི་ལྟ་བུ་ཞིག་འདུག༔ ཐ་དད་འདུག་ན་བྱུང་གནས་འགྲོ་གསུམ་ཡོག་གཅིག༔ དཔྱོད་མཁན་ཡོག་གཅིག་སོ་སོར་སྣང་ཡང་༔ སྣང་མཁན་དེ་ཉིད་ཡོད་མེད་སོགས་དབྱེ་བ་མེད་པ་སེམས་ཉིད་གཅིག་པུའི་ཀློང་དུ་བློ་ཐག་མ་ཆོད་ཀྱི་བར་དུ་ནན་ཞར་ལ་འབད་ནས་ཐག་ཆོད་པར་བྱའོ༔ དང་པོ་བྱུང་ས་མ་རྙེད་པས་སྐྱེ་མེད་ངོ་བོ་སྟོང་པ་ཆོས་སྐུ༔ བར་དུ་གནས་ས་མ་རྙེད་པས་འགག་མེད་རང་བཞིན་གསལ་བ་ལོངས་སྤྱོད་རྫོགས་སྐུ༔ ཐ་མ་འགྲོ་ས་མེད་

པར་གནས་མེད་ཐུགས་རྗེ་སྤྲུལ་པའི་སྐུ་སྟེ༔ སྐུ་གསུམ་གྱི་རང་ངོ་འཕྲོད་པའི་
ངང་ཅུང་ཟད་ངལ་བསོས་ནས་བསྒོམ་རྒྱུ་རྡུལ་ཙམ་མེད་པའི་ངང་ལ་མཉམ་པར་
བཞག་པའི་ངང་རྣམ་པར་རྟོག་པ་སྔར་འདས་པའི་རྗེས་མི་དཔྱད༔ མ་འོངས་
པའི་མདུན་མི་བསུ༔ ད་ལྟ་སྐད་ཅིག་མ་ལ་སྟོང་པ་རེད་བསམ་པའི་བློས་མི་
བྱེད༔ རྣམ་རྟོག་བཟང་པོ་མ་སྒྲུབས༔ ངན་པ་མ་འགགས༔ གང་ཤར་
ཅིར་སྣང་ཐམས་ཅད་རང་ཤར་རང་གྲོལ་གཉེན་པོས་མ་བཅོས་མ་བསླད་ཅིང་རང་
བབས་སུ་འཇོག་པ་ནི་གནས་དམ་པའོ༔ སེམས་སྦྱངས་ཉམས་ལེན་དང་པོ་
རྫོགས་སོ༔ གཉིས་པ་དངོས་གཞི་ཐུན་མོང་སེམས་སྦྱངས་ལ་བརྟེན་པ་ཆེར་
ཐོབ་ནས༔ ཐུན་མིན་ཀ་དག་ཁྲེགས་ཆོད་ཀྱི་གདམས་པ་ལ༔ རིག་པ་
གཅེར་མཐོང་གི་གནད་གཏན་ལ་དབབ་པར་བྱའོ༔ ཀུན་རྫོབ་ཀྱི་རྟོག་ངོར་
ཐོག་མར་རང་གི་སྤྱི་བོར་པད་ཟླའི་གདན་ལ་དྲིན་ཅན་རྩ་བའི་བླ་མ་བཞུགས་པར་
མོས་ལ་གསོལ་བ་ནན་གྱིས་བཏབ༔ བླ་མ་འོད་དུ་ཞུ་རང་དང་གཉིས་མེད་
འདྲེས༔ དོན་དམ་རིག་པ་སྟོང་གསལ་གྱི་གཤིས་ཀློང་ལས་བླ་མའོ་སྙམ་པའི་
རྣམ་པར་རྟོག་པ་རང་སར་དུ་རང་སྟོང་གཤིས་བརྗོད་དུ་མེད་དེ་ཐུགས་ཡིད་གཅིག་
ཏུ་འདྲེས་པ་རིག་པའི་རྩལ་ཆེན་རྫོགས་པའི་གནད་ཟབ་ཡིན་པ་ཨྠིི༔ ལུས་མི་
འགྱུར་བ་རི་བོ་ཅོག་བཞག་གི་གཞི་བཟུང་བ་ནི༔ ལུས་རྣམ་སྣང་གི་ཆོས་
བདུན་ལྡན་ནམ༔ སེམས་ཉིད་ངལ་བསོ་གང་རུང་ལས་གཡོ་འགུལ་ཐམས་
ཅད་བྲལ་བ་རི་བོ་ལྷུན་ཆགས་པ་ལྷུ་བྱུར་རང་བབས་སུ་ཅོག་གེར་སྡོད༔ མིག་
གྱི་གྱུར་མི་བྱ་བ་རྒྱ་མཚོ་ཅོག་བཞག་གིས་ཨར་ལ་གཏད་པ་ནི༔ ངག་སྨྲ་
བརྗོད་སྤུགས་བཟླས་རླུང་སོགས་རྩོལ་བ་གང་ཡང་མི་བྱེད་པར་ཁ་སོ་མ་རེག་
ཙམ་རླུང་དལ་བུས་བྱུར་འཛིན་དང་བཅས་རྩོལ་མེད་ལ་བསླབས་ནས༔ མིག་
ཟླུམ་འཁྲིལ་བར་སྣང་ལ་གཡོ་འགུལ་མེད་པར་མདུང་ཚུགས་སུ་གཏད༔

སེམས་ལས་འདས་པའི་རིག་པ་ཅིག་བཞག་གིས་གཏན་ལ་དབབ་པར་བྱ་བ་ནི༔
སེམས་མ་རིག་པ་དེ་མདོར་ན་ཡེངས་པ་དང་འཁྲུལ་པ་རྒྱུ་འབྱམས་སུ་སོང་བ་
འདིའོ༔ སེམས་བྱུང་གི་རྟོག་ཚོགས་ནི༔ སྔར་འདས་པའི་རྗེས་དཔྱད༔
མ་འོངས་པའི་མདུན་བསུ༔ ད་ལྟ་ཡིན་མིན་རྣམ་རྟོག་ཉི་ཟེར་གྱི་རྡུལ་ལྟ་བུ་
འདི་ཡིན༔ སེམས་མ་རིག་པ་ལས་འདས་པའི་རང་གི་རིག་པ་ཡེ་གདོད་མའི་
ཤེས་པ་བྱིང་རྨུག་འཐིབས་གསུམ་བདེ་གསལ་མི་རྟོག་སོགས་ཉམས་དང་མྱོང་བ་
ངེས་ཤེས་སོགས་གང་གི་ཀྱང་མ་གོས་པ་མ་བསླད་པ༔ སྟོང་ཞིང་གསལ་ལ་
འཛིན་པ་མེད་པ་ཕྱི་ནང་གང་ལའང་ཟང་ཐལ་ལེ་བ༔ སྨྲ་བརྗོད་ཀྱི་ཡུལ་ལས་
འདས་པ་འདིའི་ངང་དུ་རྩོལ་མེད་ཀྱི་དྲན་པས་ཆོས་ཟད་དུ་ལ་བཟླ་བའོ༔ རྩལ་
གྱི་འཆར་སྒོ་ཚོགས་དྲུག་གི་ཡུལ་དང་ཡུལ་ཅན་དུག་གསུམ་དུག་ལྔ་སོགས་རྟོག་
ཚོགས་ཇི་ལྟར་ཤར་ཡང་༔ ཀ་དག་གི་ལྟ་བའི་ཀློང་དུ་རྩོལ་མེད་དུ་བསྒོམ་
པས་རང་བཞིན་དུ་ཤར༔ རང་བཞིན་དུ་གྲོལ་བ་ལས་ངོ་བོ་དང་རང་རྩལ་
གཉིས་སུ་མི་བྱེད་བློས་བྱས་ཀྱི་བཟོས་པའམ༔ ཡིད་དཔྱོད་སོགས་གང་ཡང་
མི་བྱ༔ བཟང་རྟོག་སྐུ་གསུམ་ཡང་མི་བསྒྲུབ༔ ངན་རྟོག་དུག་ལྔ་ཡང་མི་
སྤང་༔ རྩོལ་སྒྲུབ་ཀྱི་མཐའ་ལས་འདས་པ་རྩོལ་མེད་ཀྱི་རིག་པ་རྒྱུད་དེད་ཀྱིས་
ཉམས་སུ་བླང་བར་བྱའོ༔ དེ་ལ་བརྟན་པ་ཆེར་ཐོབ་ནས་ལུས་རྩོལ་བཅས་
སམ༔ རྩོལ་མེད་ཀྱི་ངང་ནས་སྒལ་ཚིགས་དྲང་པོར་བསྲངས༔ མིག
ཟླུམ་འཁྲིལ་ནམ་མཁའ་ལ་མདུང་ཚུགས་སུ་གཏད༔ ངག་རྩོལ་མེད་ཕྱིར་
འཛིན་བཅས་རང་བབས་སུ་བཞག༔ རིག་པ་སྐྱེ་འགག་གནས་གསུམ་དང་
བྲལ་བར་དབྱིངས་རིག་དབྱེར་མེད་ཁྱབ་གདལ་ཆེན་པོ་རྒྱ་གར་ཡང་མ་ཆད༔
ཕྱོགས་གར་ཡང་མ་ལྷུང་བ༔ བཟོ་མེད་ཡང་དག་གི་དྲན་པས་ས་ལེར་བཞག
པས་དང་ལ་རྩལ་གྱི་འཆར་སྒོ་ཇི་ལྟར་འཆར་ཡང་༔ ཤར་ཡུལ་གྱི་ངོ་བོ་སྟོང་

གསལ་ཤར་རྒྱུའི་རྣམ་རྟོག་སྟོང་པ༔ མདོར་ན་སྟོང་པ་ལ་སྟོང་པ་ཐིམ་པས་
ཤར་གྲོལ་རྣམ་དབྱེ་དུས་མཉམ་ལ་སོང་བས་སྣང་སྲིད་འཁོར་འདས་ཀྱི་ཆོས་
ཐམས་ཅད་རེ་དོགས་དགག་སྒྲུབ་གང་ཡང་མེད་པའི་ཀ་དག་ཁྲེགས་ཆོད་ཀྱི་ཆོས་
ཟད་ལ་བཟླའོ༔ གསུམ་པ་རྗེས་འབྲས་བུ་གཏན་ལ་ཕབ་ཚུལ་ནི༔ མདོར་
ན་བདག་གཞན༔ སྣོད་དང་བཅུད༔ འཁོར་བ་དང་མྱང་འདས༔ ཕྱི་
སྣང་བའི་ཡུལ་དང་སྲིད་ཚད༔ ནང་འཛིན་པའི་སེམས་ཉིད༔ སེམས་མ་
རིག་པ་དང་སེམས་བྱུང་གི་མཚན་མ་རེ་དོགས་དགག་སྒྲུབ་སྤང་བླང་གཉེན་པོ་ཆེ་
ཕྲ་སོགས་གཉིས་བསྡུས་ཀྱི་ཆོས་ཐམས་ཅད་ཀ་ནས་དག་ཅིང་༔ ཆོས་ཉིད་
རྫོགས་པ་ཆེན་པོའི་ཀློང་དུ་ཟད་ནས་ཤར་རྒྱུའི་རྒྱུ་དང་༔ ཤར་ས་ཡུལ་གཉིས་
པོ་ནམ་མཁའ་ལ་རི་མོ་བྲིས་པ་བཞིན་མཉམ་ཁད་དུ་སོང་ནས་སྤུར་འདས་པ་མ་
འོངས་ད་ལྟ་སོགས༔ དུས་གསུམ་གྱིས་མཚོན་ཡད་རིང་གི་ཉིན་འདི༔ དོ་
ནུབ་ཀྱི་མཚན་མོ་འདི༔ མཚན་མོའི་དུས་འདས་པ་ཉིན་མོའི་སྣང་བ་ཁྲ་ལམ་
ལམ༔ འོད་འཁྱིལ་འཁྱིལ་འགྲོ་འདུག་བྱ་སྤྱོད་འདི་ལྟ་བུ་ཡིན་སྙམ་པའི་འདུ་
ཤེས་ཀྱི་བློ་དང་༔ མ་འོངས་དོ་ནུབ་ཀྱི་སྣང་བ་ནག་ཆོམ་ཆོམ༔ དོག་མེར་
མེར་ཉལ་འདུག་སོགས་འདི་ལྟ་བུའོ་སྙམ་པའི་འདུ་ཤེས་ཀྱི་བློ་ཐམས་ཅད་རིག་པ་
ཀ་དག་གི་དབྱིངས་སུ་ཐིམ་པས༔ ཉིན་མཚན་གྱི་དབྱེ་བ་མེད༔ འགྲོ་སའི་
ཡུལ་དང་འགྲོ་མཁན་གྱི་གང་ཟག༔ སྤྱོད་ཡུལ་ཕ་མ་རྒྱལ་ཁམས་སོགས་
འདི་ལྟར་ཡིན་ནོ་སྙམ་པའི་བློ་ཡི་འཛིན་པའི་འདུ་ཤེས་ཐམས་ཅད་ཀ་དག་བརྗོད་
མེད་དབྱིངས་སུ་ཐིམ་ནས་ངོ་མི་ཤེས་ཤིང་བློ་ཡི་ཡུལ་ལས་འདས་པ་རྩོལ་བཅས་
རྩོལ་མེད་སོགས་དྲན་པ་སྐྱོང་མཁན་དང་སྐྱོང་རྒྱུའི་ངོ་བོ་དང་རང་རྩལ་གསུམ་གྱི་
ཆ་དེ་ཡང་མཉམ་དག་སོང་ནས༔ གསལ་ཞིང་སྟོང་སྟོང་ཞིང་གསལ༔
གསལ་སྟོང་རིག་པའི་སྙིང་པོ་ཅན་དུས་གསུམ་དུས་མེད་གཤིས་ཐོག་ཏུ་འཕོ་

འགྱུར་མེད་པའི་ངང་དེར་ཉིན་མོ་བདག་གཞན་གྱི་འདུ་ཤེས༔ མཚན་མོ་འཁྲུལ་པའི་རྨི་ལམ༔ མ་འཁྲུལ་པའི་ཉམས་མྱོང་གི་འོད་གསལ་མཉམ་དག་ཏུ་སོང་བ༔ ཉལ་མི་ཉལ་གྱི་དབྱེ་བ་ངོ་མི་ཤེས་ཤིང་༔ བློ་ལས་འདས་པ་ཟང་ཐལ་དབྱིངས་རིག་དབྱེར་མེད་དུ་སེམས་བདལ་གྱིས་སོང་བ་འདི་ཀ་དག་ཁྲེགས་ཆོད་ཀྱི་འབྲས་བུ་གཏན་ལ་ཕབ་པའོ༔ དེ་ལྟ་བུའི་ཉམས་ལེན་མཐར་ཕྱིན་པའི་རྣལ་འབྱོར་རབ༔ སྐྲ་སེན་ཙམ་སླིགས་མ་ལྷག་མ་ལ་བཞག་ནས༔ དྭངས་མའི་ལུས་རྡུལ་ཕྲན་དུ་དེངས༔ རིག་པ་གདོད་མའི་དབྱིངས་ནང་གསལ་གཞོན་ནུ་བུམ་པའི་སྐུའི་སྦུབ་ཀློང་ལ༔ གཞི་སྣང་རིག་པར་ཐིམ་ནས་ཆོས་ཀྱི་སྐུ་རུ་སངས་རྒྱས་པ་ཡིན་ནོ༔ སླར་ཀ་དག་གདོད་མའི་དབྱིངས་ལས་ལྷུན་གྱིས་གྲུབ་པའི་གཟུགས་སྐུ་རྣམ་པ་གཉིས་རྩོལ་མེད་དུ་འབྱུང་ཞིང་༔ སྐད་ཅིག་མ་རེ་ལ་འགྲོ་བའི་དོན་དུ་སྤྲུལ་པ་བྱེ་བ་ཁྲི་ཚོ་བརྒྱ་རེ་འབད་མེད་དུ་འབྱེད་ཅིང་༔ འཁོར་བ་དོང་ནས་སྤྲུགས་པར་འགྱུར་རོ༔ དབང་པོ་འབྲིང་དཔེ་ཉི་ཟླ་འཆར་ནུབ་ཀྱི་སངས་རྒྱས་ཚུལ་ནི༔ ཆོས་བཅོ་ལྔའི་ཉི་མ་ཡོལ་བ་དང་ཟླ་བ་ཤར་བ་དུས་མཚུངས་པ་བཞིན་རྣལ་འབྱོར་པ་ལུས་རྒྱ་ཞིག་པ་དང་༔ ཀ་དག་གདོད་མའི་དབྱིངས་སུ་ཐིམ་པ་དུས་མཉམ་དུ་སོང་ནས་སྐད་ཅིག་མ་རེ་ལ་སྤྲུལ་པ་གྲངས་མེད་པས་འཁོར་བ་དོང་ནས་སྤྲུགས་པར་འགྱུར་རོ༔ དབང་པོ་ཐ་མ་བར་དོ་དང་པོ་ལ་གྲོལ་ཚུལ་ནི༔ སྤྲུལ་ཤུབ་ནས་ཐོན་པ་ལྟ་བུ་གང་ཟག་དེ་འཆི་ནད་ཀྱིས་བཏབ་ནས་ས་ཆུ་མེ་རླུང་རིམ་པ་བཞིན་དུ་ཐིམ་ནས་ཕྱི་དབུགས་ཆད་ནས༔ སྣང་བ་མཆེད་པ༔ མཆེད་པ་ཐོབ་པ་ལ་ཐིམ་ནས་ནང་དབུགས་ཆད་ནས་གཞི་ཡི་འོད་གསལ་མ་ལྟ་བུ་དང་༔ ཉམས་སུ་བླང་བའི་ཉམས་མྱོང་གི་འོད་གསལ་བུ་ལྟ་བུ་གཉིས་དབྱེར་མེད་དུ་ཐིམ་ནས་ཡང་སངས་རྒྱས་ནས་སྤྲུལ་པ་དང་འགྲོ་དོན་འབད་རྩོལ་མེད་པ་ལྷུན་གྱིས་འགྲུབ་པར་འགྱུར་

རོ༔ དབང་པོ་ཡང་མཐའ་བར་དོ་ཐ་མ་ལ་མ་པང་བུ་འཇུག་པ་ལྟ་བུ་གྲོལ་ཚུལ་ནི༔ དཔེར་ན་བུ་ཡིས་མ་ཡིན་མིན་གྱིས་བརྟག་དཔྱད་མི་དགོས་པ་ལྟར་མ་དང་བུ་འཕྲད་པ་བཞིན་དུ༔ ལྷུན་གྲུབ་བར་དོའི་སྣང་འོད་ཟེར་གསུམ་ཐིག་ལེ་ཐིག་ཕྲན་ཞི་དྲག་གི་སྐུ་ཇི་ལྟར་ཤར་ཡང་རིག་པའི་རང་རྩལ་ཡིན་པ་དང་༔ ངོ་ཤེས་པར་དུ་ཡིད་ཆེས༔ ཐ་མ་སྐུ་དེ་ཉིད་ལ་ཐིམ་ནས་མངོན་པར་རྫོགས་པར་སངས་རྒྱས་སོ༔ ཤིན་ཏུ་དབང་རྟུལ་རྣམས་ནི་རྫོགས་པ་ཆེན་པོའི་སྨིན་བྱེད་ཀྱི་དབང་གྲོལ་བྱེད་ཀྱི་ཁྲིད་ཐོབ་ནས་བརྩོན་འགྲུས་ཤིན་ཏུ་དབེན་པའི་གང་ཟག་དེ༔ བླ་མ་དང་ཆོས་ལ་དམ་ཚིག་ཕྱི་ནང་གསང་གསུམ་སེལ་མ་ཞུགས་པའི་གང་ཟག་ཤིན་ཏུ་ཐ་མལ་པ་ཡང་བླ་མ་བརྒྱུད་པའི་བྱིན་རླབས་དང་༔ རྫོགས་པ་ཆེན་པོ་བསླུ་མེད་མཐོང་གྲོལ་གྱི་ཆོས་ཡིན་པས༔ རིགས་དྲུག་དང་ངན་སོང་གི་སྐྱེ་སྒོ་ཆོད་ནས༔ མིག་འཕྲུལ་ལྟ་བུའི་སྤྲུལ་པའི་ཞིང་ཁམས་ལྔ་ལ་མེ་ཏོག་པདྨའི་སྦུབས་ལས་རྫུས་ཏེ་སྐྱེ་བ་བླངས་ནས་སངས་རྒྱས་ཀྱི་ཞལ་མཐོང་གསུང་ཐོས་བྱང་ཆུབ་སེམས་དཔའི་ཐེག་པ་ལ་ཞུགས་ནས་ཤེས་བྱའི་སྒྲིབ་པ་ཐམས་ཅད་རིམ་གྱི་དག་ནས་སངས་རྒྱས་པར་འགྱུར་རོ༔ མདོར་ན་གེགས་སེལ་བོགས་འདོན་ཐམས་ཅད་ནི༔ བླ་མ་ལ་མོས་གུས་དང་གསོལ་འདེབས་ལ་རག་ལས་པས༔ བསམ་རྒྱུ་བླ་མ་དྲན་རྒྱུ་བླ་མ་ལས་མེད་པར་མིག་མཆི་མ་མི་སྐམ་པར་རྣམ་པ་ཀུན་ཏུ་གསོལ་འདེབས་ལ་བརྩོན་པར་བྱའོ༔ ཞེས་པ་འདི་འང་གངས་རི་མཐོན་མཐིང་རྒྱལ་མོའི་འདབས༔ ༸རྗེ་བཙུན་རིན་པོ་ཆེའི་སྒྲུབ་གནས་ཤེལ་ཕུག་ཆུ་ཤིང་རྫོང་དུ་༸ཨོ་རྒྱན་རིན་པོ་ཆེའི་བྱིན་རླབས་ལ་བརྟེན་ནས་དབྱིངས་རིག་ཁྱབ་བརྡལ་གྱི་སྒྲོམ་བུ་ལས༔ དཔའ་བོ་རིག་རྩལ་ཐོགས་མེད་ཀྱིས་གཏན་ལ་ཕབ་སྟེ་བརྗོད་པའོ༔ དབྱིངས་རིག་དབྱེར་མེད་ལས་ཤར་བའི་བརྡ་ལས་གཞི་བྱས་རང་གི་ཉམས་ཀྱིས་ཟུར་བརྒྱན་ཏེ་བྲིས་པས་གང་ཟག་སྐལ་ཅན་

དབང་རྗོན་ལྷ་བདུན་ཙམ་མིན་པ་ཀུན་གྱི་སྤྱོད་ཡུལ་མ་ཡིན་པས་བཀའ་རྒྱ་ཤིན་ཏུ་དམ་པ་ཨྠྀཿ བཀའ་འདི་སྤྱགས་སྲུང་ཨེ་ཀ་ཛཱ་ཏི་དང་རེ་མ་ལ་གཏད་པ་ཡིན་པས་སྲུངས་ཤིག༔ དམ་མེད་ཀྱི་ལག་ཏུ་མ་ཤོར་ཅིག༔ གུ་ཧྱ༔

INDEX